Innovating the Design Process

Innovating the Design Process: A Theatre Design Journey explores the process of designing for theatre and details how each part of a designer's own process, no matter what their design specialization, can be innovated and adapted for a more confident journey and for better outcomes.

The book observes and deconstructs the processes used by theatre designers, uncovers and explains the structure and concepts behind those processes and shows how they can be easily reassembled for better results and to meet different situations. It uses innovative real-world practical examples from all the fields of theatre design taken from shows throughout the author's career. The processes covered in this book are split into two sections—design development and design implementation—with an additional chapter covering design presentations. Written in an engaging and informative style, this text opens up a designer's ability to innovate within the design process to optimize reproducibility, resilience, personal fit, confidence, collaboration and audience engagement.

Innovating the Design Process is a next level book for both MFA theatre design students and early career professionals who wish to develop their craft further. Seasoned professionals will also find within its pages concepts to reinvigorate their own design process.

The book includes access to an online guide to using Microsoft Word for Mac to mirror content in two separate documents.

Professor David E. Smith is a sound designer, composer, inventor, educator and author. He spent eight years with the Royal National Theatre in London, England where he engineered and designed the sound for many shows. More recently David has composed and/or designed the sound at Triad Stage in Greensboro NC, Arena Stage in Washington

DC (Helen Hayes award nomination), North Shore Music Theatre in Beverly Massachusetts, Trinity Repertory Theatre in Providence RI, The Alliance Theatre in Atlanta GA, Twin City Stage in Winston-Salem NC, Paper Lantern Theatre Company in Winston-Salem NC and Cape Fear Regional Theatre in Fayetteville NC. David is the founding director of the University of North Carolina School of the Arts BFA and MFA theatre sound design programs, where he built a unique pedagogy for training young professionals and has published papers on the intersection of audience engagement and design.

Innovating the Design Process

A Theatre Design Journey

DAVID E. SMITH

LONDON AND NEW YORK

Cover image: © Gareth Rockliffe

First published 2022
by Routledge
605 Third Avenue, New York, NY 10158

and by Routledge
4 Park Square, Milton Park, Abingdon, Oxon, OX14 4RN

Routledge is an imprint of the Taylor & Francis Group, an informa business

© 2022 David E. Smith

The right of David E. Smith to be identified as author of this work has been asserted in accordance with sections 77 and 78 of the Copyright, Designs and Patents Act 1988.

All rights reserved. No part of this book may be reprinted or reproduced or utilised in any form or by any electronic, mechanical, or other means, now known or hereafter invented, including photocopying and recording, or in any information storage or retrieval system, without permission in writing from the publishers.

Trademark notice: Product or corporate names may be trademarks or registered trademarks, and are used only for identification and explanation without intent to infringe.

Library of Congress Cataloging-in-Publication Data
A catalog record for this title has been requested

ISBN: 978-1-032-12119-2 (hbk)
ISBN: 978-1-032-12118-5 (pbk)
ISBN: 978-1-003-22316-0 (ebk)

DOI: 10.4324/9781003223160

Typeset in Dante and Avenir
by KnowledgeWorks Global Ltd.

Access the Support Material: www.routledge.com/9781032121185

The content in chapters 1, 2, and 3 has been adapted from the online paper "Innovating the Design Process - Part 1," available at https://www.usitt-sound.org/2021/03/07/innovating-the-design-process-part-1/

moon and stars
.... and fireflies

Contents

Acknowledgments ix

1 Introduction: Innovation and Creativity 1

2 Prototyping as Design Process 7

3 Words as Pre-Prototype 15

4 Script as Machine 21

5 Symbols, Narrative and Vocabulary 28

6 Granularization 36

7 Purpose, Meaning, Reason and Research 41

8 Word-Based Prototype Template 47

9 Simplicity, Syncing Up and Annealing 58

10 On-Ramp, Quest and Warm-Up 65

11 Meet & Greet 73

12	Designer Run	79
13	Next Morning	83
14	Fade Ins and Outs	91
15	Designer as Chef	98
16	Content, Distribution, Environment	104
17	Quiet Time	110
18	Tech	114
19	Observing	121
20	Ending Safely	128
	Index	135

Acknowledgments

This book has been on the back burner for decades and has taken many forms and rewrites during its gestation up to this point. It is easy to tie yourself up into knots while trying to think and write about these things. I am constantly asking myself "is that what is really going on here" and "is this what I really think about it". Being the observer and the observed at the same time is a recipe for self-doubt and confusion. However, I am very lucky to have had different people around me who have always been loving, supportive and encouraging as well as having people around me who have given me experiences in which to draw from and clarity with which to see. Still others have shown me a level of excellence I should strive for in all my undertakings. In their own individual way, they have all contributed to this book and so I would like to take the following pages to acknowledge some of them.

Firstly, and foremost, I would like to thank my darling wife and artist Diane Demers-Smith. Her love and support and boundless enthusiasm have buoyed everything I have undertaken since we met and married. My move to the USA, my career as an independent theatre designer, my teaching at UNCSA, my service and leadership within USITT and OISTAT, my inventing and patents, my entrepreneurship and involvement within the startup community and my service and leadership to both the arts and creative communities here in Winston-Salem, NC. I could not have done any of these things without her at my side. I would also like to acknowledge how she has helped this book in a very specific way. Since she is an incredible ceramics and watercolor artist[1], over the decades, I have got to witness and live through all her successes, as well as her trials and tribulations. Since we share everything, it has allowed me to observe and discuss her process as an artist up close. This has given me a level of clarity about design that I could not have gained in any other way. It distilled for me the process of a designer as something very distinct and different from the process of that of an artist even though both are creative. As you will realize, I literally could not have written this book without her!

I must draw your attention to the cover and the amazing image by my longest and best friend Gareth Rockliffe. I cannot thank him enough for allowing me to use one of his beautiful works of photographic art for the book. Our house is filled with his work as well as the haunting work of his photographer wife Jan Soderquist. One of Gareth's massive brooding coastlines hangs by our bed and is the last thing I see at night and the first thing I wake up to in the morning. Art makes you want to look not just to see. Looking is a good way to start and end your day even if at times you don't see clearly. Since the book alludes to the larger topic of design process in general, even though the examples I use are from my experience in theatre design, I didn't want an image of a theatre or a production on the cover. I wanted something more expansive and contemplative—something more universal. Civilization first developed in this littoral landscape that his art captures. I hope you will agree that his image is stunning. He has been another person who has always been there and encouraged and supported me since we met when we were 18 years old.

I owe an immense amount of thanks and gratitude to my former colleague and friend at UNCSA Dean Wilcox and my longtime friend and colleague from USITT and Cornish College of the Arts Dave Tosti-Lane. They both slogged their way through numerous early drafts of this book, giving me suggestions and helping me clarify what it was that I wanted to express. I just can't tell you how important it is to have people on your side who are willing to get down into the weeds with you and help. I used to devour Dave Tosti-Lane's articles in Mix magazine before I ever got to meet him in person. I also want to thank his wife Linda for allowing him to take time away from his *busy* retirement to do this. Additionally, Dean Wilcox was one of those other *enlightened* faculty that helped teach the Innovation and Creativity class with me even though he technically was not faculty as he was the Dean of the Division of Liberal Arts at UNCSA. His doctoral thesis was in Semiotics, and he really helped clarify the section that discusses *baggage*. He is a theatre lighting designer, so he also kept me honest when speaking for them.

Being a dean is all consuming, so I also want to thank his wife Sherri for allowing him to use some of his precious free time to undertake this work for the book.

A huge amount of thanks goes to Stacey Walker the Publisher of Audio, Theatre & Performance Studies at Routledge. She took the idea for this book and encouraged me to finish it and publish it. Initial reviews of the book proposal quoted that *no one else is writing about this stuff*. This means it is either prescient or misguided. Time will ultimately tell, but she had the courage to run with this book and for that I will be forever grateful. We live in a world of remote communication and sometimes it is hard to get a sense of a person from just emails. Her warmth and encouragement have always shone through her communications, and I hope to one day meet her to thank her in person.

As part of the publishing process, a lot of people get to work behind the scenes and I would like to also take this opportunity to thank them all. Unfortunately, I will never get to learn most of their names but I do want to thank Lucia Accorsi the senior editorial assistant at Taylor & Frances who has been working with me, month by month, keeping me on track through this new and often confusing process. Final manuscripts also get reviewed anonymously. I don't know who the external technical reviewers were, but I would like to also thank them for their comments, insight and suggestions. They pointed out sections that still needed clarification and allowed me to further refine the book. On that note, any mistakes are wholly of my own doing and come with an implicit apology. Now that this manuscript has reached the production part of the process, I would also like to acknowledge and thank Suzanne Pfister and her team from KnowledgeWorks Global Ltd.

This may be the only book I write. Considering how long I have been working on it, it may be a while before I write about all the other things that I haven't covered in this book that still need to be brought to light and discussed. Because of this, I would like to use this opportunity to thank all those who have influenced my development and career up until this point of being able to write about this subject.

Obviously, I would like to thank my father and my late mother. The experience of living all over the world with Cable & Wireless and embracing different cultures as a child made it seem like a normal thing to do. We have extended family in one of those places, Barbados, and that experience also enriched my younger life. I would also like to thank my sisters, Alison and Jenny, for putting up with me. Even they will agree that I have got a lot better with age! The pandemic has upset things recently but before it hit and travel became difficult, Diane and I would really enjoy staying with my younger sister in the UK and seeing the rest of the family, the kids and grandkids at her summer garden parties and at Christmas time. These visits always included a week wandering around English country gardens. Something I am also missing terribly during this period of isolation.

There are points of inflection in people's lives that make a big impact on how the future unfolds. I have had three of those points in my career and I would like to thank the people that made them happen. The first was the late Dr. Derek Hyde at Nonington College in the UK. Having spent a year as a street musician in France, I decided to get my act together and come back to the UK and enroll in a university. I was a late applicant, so I had to interview during the summer recess when the college was closed. A man in scrappy gardening clothes picked me up from the railway station and drove me to the campus to interview. He didn't introduce himself formally, so I thought he was just the gardener or a custodian. He was really nice, and we chatted amiably while we drove. I shared with him how apprehensive I was about being accepted, as although I had the required academic grades, I really did not have the required music credentials. I only had a history of writing songs and performing on the street and in clubs. After meetings with the principle and then the bursar etc. I was then shuffled into this light filled music room where a now appropriately dressed Dr. Derek Hyde head of the music program and overall head of the Performing Arts degree proceeded to interview and audition me. I was mortified. As you can imagine I was more than nervous, and consequently, my playing and singing left something to be desired. I suppose because of my earlier candor and the fact that they were desperate to recruit men for the program, he offered me a place in what was to be the first year of the first Performing Arts degree in the UK. He told me that he would accept me on the understanding that at the end of the first year I caught up with the other students. Whether I did or not is debatable, but he did allow me to stay and complete the degree. He gave me a chance which changed my life and for that, I will be eternally grateful.

My three years at Nonington were transformative so I really must also thank the whole college. Derek and also John Wright who headed up movement studies, the only other program in the college, were such empathetic and enlightened individuals. Their generous and encouraging leadership pervaded everything we did and certainly influenced all of us students. One particular class had a lasting impact on me from that time. For all three years, we all had to attend Theatre & Performance

Studies that combined all the three majors of music, drama and dance. It was team taught by Derek Hyde from music, Phil Thomas and Ken Pickering from drama, Chris Challis and Margot Sunderland from dance and Richard Hazelwood our resident philosopher. As well as discussing each individual artform, it highlighted opera as a unifying artform that combined all three disciplines and introduced texts that contextualized all three in a kind of overall gestalt. Susanne Langer's *Feeling and Form* was all the rage back then. I fully admit that a lot of it was over my head at the time, but the seed was planted that leads directly to this book. It opened my eyes to looking at things from a much larger perspective while also being immersed in my own specialization. I know I wasn't their best student, but these were the best professors, and they deeply influenced my process. Sadly, most of these enlightened individuals have now passed, but their spirit will forever live on in all those minds and hearts they touched.

As a coda, Nonington College was closed by Margaret Thatcher not long after the start of the Preforming Arts Degree and subsequently turned into a women's prison. As the saying goes "If not art, then what are we fighting for?"[2] Because, like Camelot, it only lasted for a short period and has seemed to have been forgotten entirely with very little trace left behind, those few of us that were students have stuck together and remained lifelong friends. I don't have the space to mention them all, but I would like to especially thank Lizzy and Martin Jenkins as well as Melanie and Symon McNie. Their friendship has always kept me in touch with the lives of the other alums and has kept the spark of Camelot alive in me from those days.

After University, I worked at the Fulcrum Center in Slough, UK where I met two other people who I would like to take this opportunity to thank for always being in my corner throughout the years. Denis Barnham and Stuart Ryding are the most irreverent and fun people to be around. They both had illustrious careers. Denis went on to work at the Royal Festival Hall, The Royal College of Art and the Royal Hospital at Chelsea the home of the Chelsea Pensioners and Stuart went on to work at Wembley and Westminster Central Hall. No matter where they worked, they always found me a seat when I couldn't afford one and also made sure I could get a haircut from Stephen Young the midnight barber after the show came down as I never could find time during the day. When our small team representing the USA arrived in Copenhagen to compete in the International Creative Business cup in 2014, Denis and Stuart were there, unannounced, waiting in the lobby of the hotel. They stayed for the whole event to support our team and encourage all the other teams. Not many friends would voluntarily travel from one country to another country to support a team from yet a different country. They are and remain the most fun and supportive friends and have always thrown the best parties.

The second point of inflection was going from The Fulcrum Center to The National Theatre (as it was then before it got its Royal charter). Tony Waldron was the head of sound at the time, and I seem to remember applying there three times before he gave me a position. Along with Tony who taught me the BBC way of soldering, interconnections and grounding, I worked in an amazing department of other sound designers who have all influenced the way I design today and the way I think about design. I would like to also thank Rob Barnard, Paul Groothuis, Paul Arditti, Christopher Shutt, Christopher Johns, Freya Edwards, Sue Patrick nee Moore (Smore), Nicola Pretious, Nick Jones, Richard Borkum and Scott Myers. I will also sneak into this list Annemarie Taylor nee Winstanley who was in costumes. They all were, and some still are, incredible designers, people and friends. At the RNT we also had to operate the shows our colleagues designed and vice versa. This gave us as designers incredible insight into how other designers design. This practice would be frowned upon these days as no designer wants to be seen to *demote* themselves to work under another designer. But the different perspective it allows without the stress of being the designer is both insightful and restorative. R&R for designers!

It is only after I left the RNT that I realized how the level of excellence of the actors, directors, composers and choreographers had also influenced me. Every show was amazing. Exceptional was normal. Just watching these people ply their craft day after day, night after night are masterclasses unto themselves. Watching them is where I started to develop my own level of granularization and desire for excellence. What's more, they were all such nice people. During the pandemic, like many other people, Diane and I have streamed a lot of BritBox and Acorn British TV shows. I see these people all the time and they are even more amazing after all these years. The last show I designed was *The Sea* by Edward Bond directed by a young Sam Mendies with Dame Judi Dench, Ken Stott, Celia Imrie, David Thewlis and a young Samuel West amongst other notables. Every show was like this. Top drawer professionals. Their exceptional quality was turtles all the way down.

The last show I worked on at the RNT was the *Richard III & King Lear* world tour. Touring with Ian McKellen was like touring with one of those great actor managers from a previous century. As well as being one of the most accomplished actors, he was also one of the most inclusive people and made us all feel like part of a special company—his company. My last vision of being part of the RNT was at a restaurant somewhere in New York after the opening night of *Richard III* at the Brooklyn Academy of Music during the after-show party. Everybody had been celebrating late into the night and were *tired and emotional*. As we sat near to Mary Soames, Winston Churchill's daughter and the chair of the RNT, Diane and I glanced over to see Ian (we referred to him as Stan in those days, for some reason) slow dancing with the director Richard Eyre on the dance floor. It struck me then… where else but with the RNT could one ever see two Knights of the realm dancing with each other while the Lady looked on[3]. As I get older, I realize how fragile and capricious decisions of employment are, so I have nothing but thanks for Tony opening the door to the transformative experience of being part of the RNT company.

The third inflection point was when I was invited to teach at UNCSA. Although Scott Templin had already been teaching some very good sound classes and they had been designing sound in student productions, they really wanted to establish their own theatre sound design BFA and MFA program. Diane Berg from the costume construction faculty spotted me as I was giving a presentation as the guest International Sound Designer at USITT in Fort Worth, Texas. The next I knew was that I was being contacted by the Dean John Sneden to come and interview with the Design & Production faculty. History played out and I was given the position and set about building a sound department and degree programs, and my life was transformed again. I learned after the fact that they had also been in discussions with both Abe Jacobs and Jonathan Deans to help establish a sound program. With this new teaching position, my insight into design also took a major step forward. Watching the students make the same mistakes and confront the same issues I had done when I was starting out allowed me to revisit how the design process worked. What was myth and what was true. Whether the students realized it or not, I was gaining as much from them while they were being taught by me, so I want to take this opportunity to thank all of you. You know who you are, and I am so proud of how successful you have all become in your careers.

Another couple instrumental in bringing me to campus were Assistant Dean John Toia and his wife Alumni Director Eva Toia. John was the director of the stage management program and is a closet sound designer. Consequently, we shared the same vision, and he was able to help me establish the program I felt was needed within all the compliance requirements of a university and consistent within the established pedagogy of the school of Design & Production. His wife Eva also helped me ground the sound program in a much larger student tradition befitting one of the top training schools in the country. Additionally, Henry Grillo (another closet audiophile), who was head of the graduate program helped me to set up the MFA degree in theatre sound design. Eva and John, Henry and his wife Kathy and Diane and I would always be around at John and Julia Sneden's celebrating every conceivable occasion. We all became like family and I want to acknowledge each of their contributions to the sound program and consequently the writing of this book. I also want to acknowledge their continuing friendship and support for me. Sadly, John and Julia Sneden are no longer with us, and Henry and Kathy have both retired, but John and Eva now work for the Philadelphia Opera and are once again blazing a trail and innovating during this period of reimagining live entertainment during a pandemic.

I would like to also acknowledge the friendship and support of all the individuals leading all the other great theatre sound programs in the USA. Sound is a small world, and even though we all ran competitive programs, we are all friends and have known and respected each other a long time. If they will forgive me, I will dispense with their professional names and titles and refer to them by how I know them all in no particular order. David Budries at Yale (and alum Brad Ward), Rick Thomas at Purdue, Eileen Smitheimer at University of Delaware, Michael Hooker and Vinnie Olivieri at UCal Irvine, Tom Mardikes at UKMC, Jon Gottlieb at Cal Arts, Curtis Craig at Penn State, Joe Pino and Sarah Pickett at Carnegie Mellon, Sunny Kil at SUNY New Platz, EunJin EJ Cho at LSU, Bill Liotta at the University of New Mexico, Dr. John Bracewell and Don Tindall at Ithaca College, Chuck Hatcher followed by Jeremy Lee at CCM, Erik Alberg at Hope College, Toy Deiorio at DePaul, Nick Drashner at Kent State and Christopher Plummer at Michigan Tech. Some of them have now moved on but during their time they were friends and colleagues. I will also include John Taylor from d&b and John Leonard the grandfather of British sound design in this list. Were they over here in the USA and had either of them run a program they would have given us all a run for our money! I would also like to acknowledge and thank Jason Romney, a graduate of my MFA program, for his years helping me run the theatre sound program and for taking it over after I retired.

Lastly (and finally), I would like to acknowledge and thank Philips Saeco Synthia and Lavazza Super Crema. Those writers that know, will understand!

Notes

1 Check out her work on Instagram @diane_artist_potter
2 A well-known saying often misattributed to Winston Churchill.
3 Saying attributed to the critic Michael Billington.

Introduction 1

Innovation and Creativity

For over a decade, I have taught a capstone class to interested BFA and MFA students in their final semester at the University of North Carolina School of the Arts (UNCSA). The essence of this *Innovation and Creativity* class is to watch documentaries and read books about other innovative and creative people or teams (creatives) and try to observe and uncover their innovative and creative processes. The class then discusses as a group what aspects could be useful to bring into the student's own personal innovative and creative process toolbox. The class includes such creatively diverse subjects and people as Black Mountain College, Twyla Tharp, Andy Goldsworthy, Evelynne Glennie, Marina Abramovic, Louis Kahn, Gerhardt Richter, The Vignellis, The Eames' and Cai Guo-Qiang amongst others.

The structure of the class is to watch the documentary and read the assigned chapter, and then come prepared for class discussion. The students also write their own notes while watching and reading, and then send them to me beforehand so I can better target my questions and know they have done the work. I originally developed the class for students in our conservatory here at UNCSA in order to give them a much wider perspective before we unleashed them upon the unsuspecting outside world. It also serves to give them practice in the skill of what Picasso described as *"stealing like an artist"*[1], not to plagiarize but to use the creativity of others to continually inspire and develop their own creative and innovative process after they graduate. I purposely try not to use the words *art* or *design* when discussing these processes, as the class is made up of students from

DOI: 10.4324/9781003223160-1

many different disciplines including technical majors and management majors, and not just designers. Not everyone sees themselves as an *artist* or *designer*, but they do feel that what they do is sometimes innovative and/or creative—hence the title. I believe that it is this myriad of diverse voices around the table from very different backgrounds that gives this class its richness.

It is surprisingly difficult to observe and uncover someone else's creative process. It is so easy to be distracted by what a creative is doing, what they are making, their tools, their surroundings, their product, whether we think they are nice, smart, kind to their partners or spouses, creative, successful... or not. Observing and uncovering is also especially difficult these days when social media commands our every waking moment. Under social media's influence, we have all been purposefully addicted to casting an opinion about everything, even the things that previously never required an opinion. These opinions don't now demand any thought or understanding and don't have need for any expertise or experience. We just have to *Like* 👍 or not as the case may be and move on as quickly as possible to cast the next opinion. The need for this next *opinion dopamine hit* is so insidious and continuous that there is no time for rumination or reflection or any sense of owning the consequences of expressing the opinion. Any flicker of guilt or responsibility is quickly ameliorated by the next *Like* 👍 with its associated little *high*. Sadly, these days, firmly held opinion seems to trump any depth of consideration, empathy or appetite for ambiguity; the very abilities that are necessary for observing and uncovering someone else's innovative and creative process. Developing and adding to one's own creative process requires observation without judgment and uncovering without immediately moving on.

Observing without judging is a hard thing for anyone to do, perhaps especially for students. My process in the class when confronted with "I like..." or "I dislike..." is to always acknowledge it and dig deeper. Why do you like or dislike? What aspect did you most like or dislike? I have to train myself to ask questions in such a way that they cannot be answered with either "I like" or "I dislike". Once the student has explained what they meant and have dug a little deeper, I always try to restate their original response. I use this new deeper explanation and show how this leads to a much more interesting conversation that can now be opened up to the wider group for further discussion. Statements such as "I like" or "I dislike" leave nowhere else for the conversation to go except agreement or disagreement, which is the antithesis of observing and uncovering.

Despite these inescapable hurdles, as a class, we discuss the material week by week over the semester. As we slowly dispense with the *drive-by* opinions and push through the *rabbit-hole* distractions, we start to unpeel the layers to uncover and dig into the different processes being practiced by these diverse creatives. It is quite transcendent for the class when we start to differentiate the process being practiced from the person, their work and their product. This requires a lot of coaxing and cajoling, and I am very fortunate these days to have some other particularly enlightened members of the faculty to help team teach the class with me, especially since the class has recently doubled in size and popularity.

As with any journey, our discussions each year take their own unique path through the same terrain. As you can imagine, we don't always uncover and discuss exactly the same processes every year. However, despite the slightly different *way* [that] *leads on to way* ... [2], what consistently becomes apparent is that it is also hard for us to observe and uncover our own creative process. The complete concentration on the task that is necessary when we are in the throes of being creative, where self-conscious actions and awareness are merged together as described by Csikszentmihalyi[3] in *Flow*, precludes any sense of being able to observe ourselves at the same time and identify the processes that we are undertaking.

If we can't easily identify process in ourselves, how can we then add to it or decide to use a different process entirely? There is this maxim that one of the signs of attaining adulthood is recognizing and accepting that other people think differently to us without us wanting to change them—a kind of recognizing and living with difference. Similarly, I believe that a sign of creative maturity is when a creative can observe their own process and change it if they want to or need to—a kind of second-order recognition and control. The Innovation and Creativity class is structured to develop this in the students. By watching and reading, they cannot change the way the creatives work, they can only observe them and then learn from their observations and apply what they have learned to their own creative and innovative processes.

In his book *Old Masters and Young Geniuses*, the author David Galenson uses the price of artwork throughout an artist's life to show that they usually fall into either of two groups. One group he terms as *conceptual* artists whose creativity develops early on in their career; and the other he calls *experimental* artists, whose creativity takes a long period of experimentation and refinement to develop. I am in that second camp. It has taken me a whole career of practicing as a designer to understand what it is I am really doing; to then take it apart, optimize each part and then reassemble my process for better results.

My career has been as that of a theatre sound designer and although some of the examples in this book reflect that experience, they are not limited by them. As with Twyla Tharp's book *The Creative Habit*, which was not just limited to dancers and choreographers, what I have learned and uncovered is about the much wider area of design, its concepts, practice and philosophy. As such, all the insights included in this book can be applied to your own field of design in whatever way you feel appropriate.

After a quarter century of observing students as an educator, I noticed that when they learn something for themselves, they do it in a very different way than we educators traditionally like to teach them. Their method seems to be much more fragmented and nonlinear, both recursive and discursive, with eventual understanding as a process of coming into focus rather than being built up brick upon brick. We have taught them well! A class may be laid out logically, progressing steadily brick upon brick from A to Z throughout the semester, but from the student's point of view of attending many different classes all at the same time, it is just a lot of disconnected fragments they are experiencing and trying to make sense of.

President Abraham Lincoln has been quoted as saying that it is much easier to ride a horse in the direction it is [already] going. To that end, what seems to be needed is something different that acknowledges the way people learn and connects these fragments and allows them to coalesce into a fabric of understanding. The Innovation and Creativity class was one attempt at providing this and the way I have chosen to write this book is another. It is unlikely that everything within these pages will be new to the reader but because it is written less like a traditional textbook and more like a conversation, a coalescing of understanding, I am hoping that the larger fabric of design process will emerge.

To honor my background, this book is laid out like a play. The first act loosely covers developing a design, then follows a short intermission which covers design presentations and finally the second act loosely covers implementing a design. In sharing my insights and experience, I have not thought of them as only limited to a certain level of designer. In university parlance, both undergraduate and graduate design students should find this book useful. However, having taught both MFA and BFA students, the value of some of what I discuss may only become apparent after a designer has had some experience in designing and has come up against the limitations of their own process. As such, I hope this book will also serve any experienced professional designer who is wishing for their process to be reinvigorated.

Within these pages, I have also consciously tried to stay away from any discussion involving technology, systems or engineering. Firstly, because it is different for each design discipline, but more importantly because its lifespan is so much shorter than the ideas and process of design contained within these pages. As such, I hope this book will serve the reader well for many years.

Words constantly evolve. As some words gain in meaning and value, other words lose it. *Recreation* is one of those words. It used to mean practicing being creative over and over again. That is the "re" part of the word. Because being creative as a child usually also meant running around while doing it, recreation evolved into meaning sports, with its current emphasis on winning and losing. There is no winning or losing when innovating and creating. There is only practice. Rather than read this book as just an intellectual exercise, I encourage you to put into practice the ideas within these pages as well as any ideas of your own they may provoke. I suggest that we take our ideas apart, modify them and reassemble them repeatedly to better suit our own processes. To judge these ideas as either winners or losers are to miss the point, they need to be practiced.

I hope this book's greatest *offering* to the wider profession of design will be to show that what was once thought of as fixed and indivisible can now be taken apart, rearranged and changed at will. We as designers can not only unlock and deconstruct the processes that other creatives use and apply them back to our own creative process, but we can also apply our own process of innovation and creativity to our own process of design. Designing design. Design squared. D^2.

Maybe there is yet a third group of creatives that Galenson has yet to identify; experimental artists who after a long career of experimentation and refinement make sense of it all by becoming conceptual artists. In a way that is what Tharp and others are becoming in their writings and presentations. It would be interesting to see if there were similar data that would support this thesis. If there were to be such a group, I would be humbled to be considered one of them.

Notes

1 Pablo Picasso is often quoted as saying: "Good artists copy, great artists steal".
2 Referencing a line from *The Road Not Taken*. A poem by Robert Frost.

3 Mihalyi Csikszentmihalyi is a psychologist who conducted a long-term study that used pagers to randomly interrupt creatives while working and report how they felt at that moment. This allowed him to uncover a focused creative state he called Flow.

References

Csikszentmihalyi, Mihaly. (1990) *Flow: The Psychology of Optimal Experience*. New York, NY: Harper and Row.
Frost, Robert. (August 1915) The Road Not Taken. *The Atlantic Monthly*.
Galenson, David. (2007) *Old Masters and Young Geniuses: The Two Life Cycles of Artistic Creativity*. Princeton, NJ: Princeton University Press.

Prototyping as Design Process   2

One of the documentaries we watch in our Innovation and Creativity class is Maya Lin's *A Strong Clear Vision* (1994) about her designing the Vietnam Veterans Memorial in Washington, D.C. I am particularly struck by the comment she made on the plane while on her way down to Alabama for her first site visit for the Civil Rights Memorial…

> [I needed to] come up with a definition in a verbal way before I found a form for it… I need to understand conceptually what the piece is about before I visit the site, because once I visit the site, I tend to start designing.

In essence, Maya Lin seems to be articulating this recognition of her creative process and her control over it. She must first recognize and then hold herself back from kicking into an automatic mode of design in order to purposefully practice a more considered process.

I personally can identify with this. As one of the designers on a theatre show, I have often been contracted at the last moment, to help a production out of a sticky situation. This is usually because either someone has dropped out at the last moment or the production has blossomed into something needing a more experienced or nuanced touch. Either way, I must hit the ground running and my automatic design process kicks in. This process obviously produces credible results otherwise I would not be employed to do such things, but I find it less than satisfying. Like other creatives, I also need my design process to *feed me* creatively so that my

DOI: 10.4324/9781003223160-2

water well of creativity doesn't run dry. Like Maya Lin, when I can, I purposefully choose a different process as I believe a better creative journey always leads to better collaboration and better outcomes.

At this point, we should also draw attention to another part of Maya Lin's quote above. She also seems to be saying that not only does she *not* kick into an automatic process of form finding using (one would imagine) visual sketches and renderings etc., but she substitutes a completely different medium in which to practice this alternative creative process. She uses the medium of verbal definition instead. She uses words and sentences, the materials of that different medium, to first prototype meaning and engagement before she finds form for it. We can see this in the documentary as she always starts her designs by asking herself what does it mean to be *such-and-such*? What does it mean to be a Civil Rights Memorial? What does it mean to be a Vietnam Veterans Memorial?

Every field of design in theatre uses a different prototyping medium than they use for the actual design. A set designer uses sketches, drawings, renderings and models to manipulate and communicate their design. The actual finished set on the stage is not made from any of these materials or mediums. A costume designer uses renderings and fabric swatches and draped muslin on a body form. Apart from the small swatches of fabric stapled to a sketch, the actual finished costume on the actor is not made of most of these materials and does not use any of these mediums. Similar observations can also be made for lighting. A gel (or color) is not the light it casts and even these days where the look of lighting can be incorporated into the Photoshop 3D walk-through rendering, the pixel image on the screen is not made of the same materials as that used on the stage. A similar argument can be made for the newest field in theatre design, that of projections.

We can quickly think of some obvious reasons for these different materials and mediums being used for prototyping a design.

- The materials cost less than the real thing.
- It takes less time to make anything using them.
- It can be made by one person.
- It is easier to change.
- It is much easier to transport to designer meetings with clients etc.

However, there are also some less obvious reasons for using a different medium and materials for a prototype. Let's explore some of them in detail.

Over the last 25 years, the West Coast design company, IDEO, has been one of the major players in moving prototyping to earlier and earlier into their process of industrial and transformational design. Historically, prototyping was very expensive and required considerable expertise, a product would only get prototyped at the end of the design process when everyone had finished deciding and had completed all the changes. A prototype was used as a confirmation tool of the final design rather than an intrinsic part of the design process itself. As materials got cheaper and fabrication techniques easier to use, people started to realize that they could make many more low-cost *rough* prototypes. Now there was potential to move prototyping to much earlier in the design process and to do it multiple times throughout the process. This encouraged the design process to move away from drilling down to a tighter and tighter specification and become instead more of a quick and iterative process based on mockups.

At this same time, another trend was also happening. The clients of these industrial designers were wanting to collaborate more and more and get their own hands dirty in the design process. Gone were the days of contracting a design company and being delivered an end-product without any input or confirmation of direction along the way. A physical prototype made from a simpler material/medium is very different from a sketch or a rendering. I may not be able to draw but I can pick up a prototype of a device that I am supposed to use and see how it feels and how it functions. It doesn't require any special ability or previous training to prod and poke something.

Additionally, the roughness and skeletal nature of prototypes usually requires a certain amount of imagination to complete. As soon as someone completes the prototype with their imagination, they have invested part of themselves in that design. They have formed some personal ownership with that design. When collaborating with many people contributing their imagination to complete the design, there is now a sense of shared ownership by the group.

Rough prototypes are less intimidating. Their simpler materials and sometimes reduced scale are immediately perceived by collaborators as being less valuable than would be the finished product. The prototype now invites being changed and rearranged to the point of even breaking them. When the company IDEO moved the generating of prototypes to earlier into the design process, the prototype also became less precious. It turns out that it is this seeming preciousness of the prototype that is intimidating when a collaborator wants to change something or break it altogether.

For instance, although we assume that it is the reduced scale of a set model that makes it a more collaborative prototype, it is really the material or medium that makes it more inviting for collaboration. In fact, the reduced scale can sometimes have the opposite effect. Frank Gehry addresses this preciousness specifically in the documentary by Sydney Pollack, *Sketches of Frank Gehry* 2006. Gehry and his design partner Craig Webb purposefully build their prototype models at different scales simultaneously to stop them from becoming *objet d'art* and too precious to change. Something is obviously less precious if there are many instances of it; think milk cartons. Also, the different scales of the instances make it even less precious as it is hard for us to assess which scale would be more precious than another.

It is this potential preciousness of the prototype that discourages client collaborations, so the answer to this issue is to make the prototype out of a conspicuously less precious medium, hence the muslin draped on a body form or a simple white foam-core or cardboard model. The obvious inexpensive material invites touch and allows for change. The prototype is not just a product, but a whole designed experience for collaboration and the perceived value of the materials and scale is just part of that designed experience.

To encourage this collaboration to happen the prototype medium should also be perceived as less involved and labor intensive. If the prototype is perceived as having taken many hours and a labor of love, then this added preciousness discourages change and, therefore, collaboration. I see this happen in a subtle way with some set designers. Some of the prototype models they produce while working in the early stages with a director are very rough without much detail and made from stiff white paper. These invite much hands-on collaboration and are constantly changed by the director and design team. Sometimes they are even broken, or pieces discarded. However, by the time we come to the *Meet & Greet* (see later) when the set design has been locked down, the set designer presents a finished foam core model with many intricate details, miniature props, actors, furniture etc., and sometimes with the walls and floor of the set rendered like the actual set would be, sitting in a black-box model of a theatre.

The set designer has now turned their prototype into this precious model like an overly ornate birthday cake that we don't want to cut into. This detailed model communicates "hands off". This is what it is, and no more changes can happen as the drawings have now been produced and the shop has already started building the set from the drawings. I have witnessed many a director after this point go back to the model to start to change something because it is not working out in rehearsals and be put off because they start to damage this precious object. What has happened is that the original rough prototype has now been transformed into a confirmatory model, which as noted above is the end of a traditional design process. Whether set designers realize this is what they are in fact doing or not, we must admit, it is a masterful move to deter changes that would now be costly and hard to implement.

Rough and early prototypes also help with the designer's own perception and organization of thoughts about the project. They allow them to take the idea out of their head and see it sitting in front of them on its own, where they (and others) can prod it and poke it and change it and rearrange it and look at it from different perspectives. This is another important aspect of turning an idea or a design into a prototype early in the process, it separates the work from the creator. If the prototype gets criticized and changed, it doesn't mean that the person whose idea it was gets criticized or their design skills challenged. Conversely, ideas that have not been prototyped just live inside the head of the originator. It is hard for that person to separate criticism of their idea from criticism of themselves. We all want our cleverness and the completeness of our creative ideas to be appreciated by others and it sometimes hurts a bit when others try to make them *even better*. Separating the idea from the person generating that idea by using rough prototypes as early as possible in the process helps designers become more objective and not take criticism of the design personally. This then allows their ideas to be refined by others.

Another aspect of this separation is by having more than one prototype. The more options that a collaborative team has in front of them (within reason), the less likely any criticism of any one of those options is felt by the original creator. This is the idea behind the design process we call brainstorming. Once again, IDEO really pioneered the increased use of brainstorming many ideas at the same time, as part of their design process they call their *Deep Dive*. For a Deep Dive, IDEO assembles a team of people with diverse backgrounds and skills, sometimes even including clients and customers. In the early stages of a Deep Dive, after each team member has reported back to the group on what they discovered during the empathy and anthropological research phase (observing and uncovering), the team then starts coming up with ideas, lots of ideas, crazy ideas, good ideas and bad ideas. Each team member coming up with an idea represents that idea by writing a brief sentence or drawing a rough diagram on a post-it note. They then briefly tell the team about their idea as they stick their post-it notes on the wall with the others. The post-it note becomes symbolic of the brief story behind it, the idea. By each member of the team coming up with many different ideas as possible and posting them on the wall, they have in effect, started to relinquish ownership of their own ideas.

IDEO takes this relinquishing of ownership a step further in the next stage of their brainstorming process. Once all the ideas have been generated, the team then groups similar ideas together and distills them into a new post-it note that now signifies the core idea of the grouping. This new distilled core idea post-it note is now not owned by any one individual but is now owned by the whole team. As we have discussed, as soon as the idea is not perceived as being owned by any one individual, it is freer to be questioned and adapted and changed by others.

A prototype, being essentially a low-value early-stage analogue of the eventual product, is also a way in its own right of conceptualizing and theorizing. It is a different way of thinking that is very much based on trial-and-error problem solving. This aspect is also alluded to in Maya Lin's comment about needing to come up with a definition in a verbal way before she found a form for it. If we further refine her use of the word *definition* to include theory and concept, then we see that prototyping, rather than just being a search for a product, a final form, is really a trial-and-error search for concept and theory on which to base that form. It recalls all those Monet paintings of haystacks. Prototyping them by painting them repeatedly under different lighting and in different weather conditions could be seen as a search for the underlying concept or theory of *Haystackness* as well as a search for diversity of form.

We have now added to the list of reasons for a more basic prototype medium. Here is the full list.

- It costs less than the real thing.
- It takes less time to use.
- It can be accomplished by one person.
- It is easier to change.
- It is much easier to transport to designer meetings etc.
- It becomes part of the creative process and not just used for confirmation at the end.
- It encourages collaboration with the client and other creatives.
- It requires imagination and personal investment to complete leading to shared ownership.
- It mitigates any preciousness that would discourage collaboration and change

- It takes less time to make… and make again.
- It separates the idea from the idea originator making any change less personal.
- It allows for many prototypes from the same idea diluting the resistance of ownership.
- It develops and becomes a symbol for the group and not just the individual.
- It is a way of thinking. A method of problem solving.

Some may have noticed that I left sound out of the list of theatre design fields earlier on. There is an insidious problem with the current process of designing sound for live drama. What is our prototype medium? "What do you mean?" we ask. "We just quickly edit it on our laptop and play it to the director". Sound has unfortunately cornered itself into a situation of having to use essentially the same material/medium for its prototyping as it does for an actual show. The problems this causes are all too evident. Let me list them.

- The sound prototype takes as much time and work to build and edit as it does to build and edit a real cue for a show.
- Even when the sound designer is brainstorming ideas themselves before any collaboration takes place, the time/work overhead involved in editing sounds, means that necessary iterations are not as plentiful or as agile.
- Because of the time and work involved to get a sound cue to where it can be played to someone else, there is no ability to move a rougher version to earlier into the design process.
- The time and work invested make the sound cue *precious* with (once again) the potential for resistance to change.
- Due to the time and work involved, it is hard to build many different sound options with its associated relinquishing of ownership.
- Since this is all done on a laptop that is either owned or being controlled by the sound designer, it works against disassociating the work from the worker with its inherent sense of shared or non-ownership which is necessary for equal status collaboration. Laptops are very personal. A director is not going to prod and poke our laptop!
- Also, since there is no sense of it being a rough early sound prototype and different from the end product, there is now no room left for a collaborator to complete the rough prototype. There is now no room for their imagination and their buying into a shared ownership of the creative process.

- Whereas a director or other designer can pick up a piece of the foam core model and move it themselves, the sound designer must do the edits for them and play back to them the altered piece. In this role, the sound designer is now acting as a sound technician/engineer, a *functionary* working for the director or other designers and not as an *equal* collaborating with them.

All these issues are caused because there is no apparent rough prototype material/medium for sound as there is with the other design fields. Or is there?

Think about the IDEO brainstorming process detailed earlier. The post-it notes contain short sentences or rough diagrams which remind the other collaborators of an idea or a fact that was contained in a short story that they were told when the idea was first presented and stuck on the wall. It is not the post-it notes that are the rough prototype medium, it is the words and the concepts and thoughts encapsulated in the story behind those words that are the real prototyping medium. The post-it notes give the ideas presentational persistence in front of us. They also allow those ideas to be moved around and rearranged to make sense of and problem solve. The post-it notes are just the vehicle for the idea using the medium of... words. Look again at Maya Lin's quote above, she says that she needed to come up with a definition in a *verbal* way before she found a form for it. Why verbal? Why words?

References

Lee Mock, F. (Director) & Sanders, T (Producer). (1994). *Maya Lin: A Strong Clear Vision*. [Motion Picture]. Washington, DC: American Film Foundation.

Pollack, S. (Director) & Guilfoyle, U. (Producer). (2006). *Sketches of Frank Gehry*. [Motion Picture]. Los Angeles, CA: Sony Picture Classics.

Words as Pre-Prototype   3

We are now at the start of Chapter 3, and I am about to state what may be the obvious. The universal shared rough prototype material/medium for all creative collaborations are… words. Words = ideas = concepts = theory behind practice.

Let's look at the pros for using words.

- *Experience.* We all have a lot of experience using words (unlike draping muslin or editing sound).
- *Agreement.* There seems to be a consensus as to what each word represents or means in context.
- *Many Choices.* If there is poor consensus, there are plenty of other words to choose from with potentially greater consensus of shared meaning.
- *Adaptable.* Words are easily changed and rearranged to help develop an idea or even completely change the idea.
- *Collaborative.* Words allow for a two-way dialogue between collaborators (whereas, not all collaborators may be skilled at other forms of physical prototyping)
- *Imagination.* Words allow room for imagination to complete the picture.
- *Low cost.* Words don't cost anything more than the original time and effort of acquiring them and don't require any specialized equipment.
- *Lingua Franca.* Words are a good choice for communicating with a director whose whole career has probably been spent using and manipulating words.

16 Words as Pre-Prototype

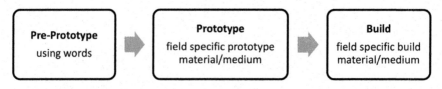

Fig 3.1. The three stages of designing a show. (Diagram showing progression from pre-prototype, through prototype to build.)

In fact, if we are honest with ourselves, each creative collaboration starts out as words anyway. The first designer meetings for the shows I get to work on are usually held around a restaurant table with the director and other designers discussing the script and the possible directions that our production could explore. All the design fields seem to intrinsically understand that these early creative explorations need to be conversations using words. Let us call this use of words to discuss ideas a *pre-prototype* material/medium. Now we can clearly see that the process of designing a show goes through three stages. First the universal shared pre-prototype using words that are common to all fields, then into each field's own specific prototyping material/medium (such as foam core models) and finally into their own specific build material/medium (such as lumber and metal) finally culminating on stage in front of an audience. See Figure 3.1.

If we now go back and reconsider the innovation that IDEO championed with respect to prototypes as discussed earlier, we see that far from inventing the prototype or the concept of prototyping, they essentially unlocked it from its traditional position. They moved it from the end of a chain of events, as part of a confirmatory process, to earlier into the actual design process. IDEO's innovation was to have the creativity to see something that was thought of as fixed and locked in sequence and move it around for better results. See Figure 3.2.

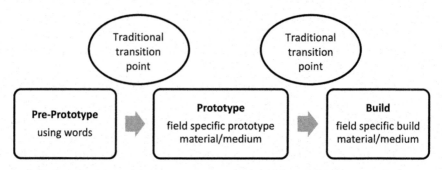

Fig 3.2. The transition points between the three stages of design. (Diagram with two transition points between each of the three stages.)

Words as Pre-Prototype 17

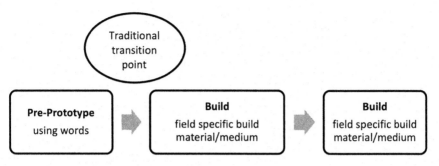

Fig 3.3. Sound design's traditional transition directly from pre-prototype to build. (Diagram with only one traditional transition point between pre-prototype and build.)

As discussed earlier, sound design does not seem to have a readily available prototype material/medium that is different in any substantial way from the build material/medium, so the pre-prototype material/medium must transition directly into the build material/medium. But where does that transition usually happen in the process of designing sound and can it be moved for better results? Traditionally, the transition happens very early on with sound. See Figure 3.3. This is evident with our educational student productions here at UNCSA. By the time a busy faculty director can take time away from the rehearsal process and classes to devote to the sound designer, they usually expect to be listening to something and not just discussing it.

This problem seems to be exacerbated unintentionally by stage management. Once rehearsals start, until the point where the director wants to meet and listen to something, the only communication from director to the sound designer has usually been through rehearsal notes such as "Bottom of Page 57. The director wants the sound of a car pulling up on Tyler's exit". As an educator, I have witnessed communications like this from both ends. In rehearsal, the actor asks… "So why does my character exit at this point and not later?" and the director muses out loud… "How about if you hear Aunt Joan's car pull up outside, would that motivate your character to exit?". The student stage manager hears this and writes it down as a statement of fact in the rehearsal notes. By the time the student sound designer reads it, it is now an instruction and has lost any sense of a request for exploration and collaboration. The student sound designer then spends countless hours building and perfecting the sound cue of a car driving up only to be told when playing cues to a director that "Oh! That was solved by another character exiting first"!

18 Words as Pre-Prototype

Thankfully, the more expert stage managers that I have worked with professionally usually change notes like this to something that encourages the continued design collaboration… "Bottom of Page 57. The director wants to explore the sound of Aunt Joan's car arriving or something else to motivate his character to exit. Can you discuss with them?". Or better still, they usually leave it out of the notes and email me directly to give me a heads-up as they realize how difficult it is working remotely. Designers usually don't get to be resident at the theatre until designer run (see later).

As discussed above, the point where prototyping sound with words ends and changes over to recording, editing and building real sound cues is usually determined by receiving a rehearsal note and not anything to do with an optimized design process. What IDEO really achieved was to move the placement of prototyping and make it rougher. This allowed the creative process to stay in the prototype phase longer because of all the benefits we have already discussed. So, the question now becomes, how can we extend the prototyping process of sound design using words, with their inherent agility and shared meaning, before transitioning to actual sound? After all, seen as part of a big picture process, the transition to building real sound cues should really be more like a confirmation phase of the process (like the pre-IDEO use of prototyping) rather than part of the creative phase. See Figure 3.4.

I have discovered that there are two approaches to extend the prototyping process using words and they both must be done together to be successful. The first more practical approach is to always respond to anything such as a rehearsal note with words and not with sounds. Simple really! The second and most important is to fully embrace manipulating words as part of our own personal design process as well as when

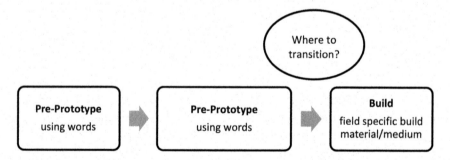

Fig 3.4. The optimal transition point from a word-based pre-prototype to a build. (Diagram with one transition point as a question between pre-prototype and build.)

collaborating with directors and other designers. Let's explore the first approach more fully before moving on to the second approach in the next chapter.

As a designer, we always need to develop a separate channel of communication with a director that does not involve any production or management personnel. Think about it. Designers have been contracted to be creative and imagine and explore with the director, whereas the role of production and management personnel is to lock things down into a list or sequence or something concrete that is achievable and within budget. If we are working remotely, this separate channel for creative communication can be done using private messaging, or private groups on social media or email or videoconference. Whatever the method is, it should be separate from one that includes any production or management personnel. As with all creative processes, we need to allow some crazy ideas to survive for a while even if they could never be achieved in order to make the leap to new original ideas that could be achieved. Any form of editing from the outside at this stage usually has the effect of dampening and lessening any creative destination.

Of course, if we are on-site, we need to cultivate some face-to-face time. We need to grab lunch with the director or buy them a coffee or have dinner with them or meet them at the bar afterwards. I am not saying we should never be in the rehearsal room, because we should if we can. But remember, in the rehearsal room, the director is wrangling numerous actors, stage managers and dramaturges, while going through their process of creative form finding with all eyes on them. It's like being a Plantagenet King on their wedding night, everyone is in their bedroom watching to see if they can perform! The pressure on the director must be enormous so their bandwidth for collaborative creative reflection and rumination is usually severely reduced. Yes, they are discovering exciting opportunities for design as they stage the play, but the rehearsal room is not usually the place to discuss it with them leisurely and expansively. Also, there are usually production and/or management personnel there within earshot which may lead to the curtailing of an idea before it has been allowed to go on a creative journey and arrive somewhere unique and achievable. Please don't misunderstand me. A good stage manager is worth their weight in gold, but they are not necessarily beneficial at this stage of the prototyping process using words.

In short, we need to develop a creative relationship with the director and other designers that has its own private channel of face-to-face or remote communication. With this in place, any rehearsal notes about sound should produce an immediate communication to clarify or explore further or offer up other ideas. In essence, to keep the prototype in the form of words and to keep it fluid and agile and not let it harden into fixed recorded/edited sound cues.

We do need to sometimes play sounds to a director, but these are better if they are not potential sound cues. Sometimes I ask my questions by playing them sounds or music. Questions like… is this the *grittiness* you were mentioning? Does this embody the *purity* you were seeking? In fact, I usually have a few diverse examples and the questions follow the form of "Which one of these sounds feels most like [whatever descriptor] you talked about". It's like those Gelato stores that give out little scoops to taste before you buy. Sometimes we just need to get the director to taste a few different gelatos before we can figure out the taste they are looking for!

That works for sound, but what about other fields of design? It is important to understand that every transition point from pre-prototype to prototype, and from prototype to build, is also a potential disruption point for collaboration. As already explained, a pre-prototype using words can include more people collaborating than can a field specific prototype material/medium. An even greater constriction in collaboration also happens in the final transition to a field specific build material/medium. Every design field can not only decide where these transitions occur to minimize any potential disruption in collaboration, but they can also choose to extend any of these stages of design (and associated wider collaboration) for better results. As you will see in the next chapter, investing in a process of pre-prototyping using words and extending that pre-prototype stage for as long as possible has not only allowed me to optimize my own design process but have revealed it as a potential design process structure for all fields of design.

Reference

Lee Mock, F. (Director) & Sanders, T (Producer). (1994). *Maya Lin: A Strong Clear Vision*. [Motion Picture]. Washington, DC: American Film Foundation.

Script as Machine   4

Have you ever worked on a new play with the playwright in the rehearsal room? What sometimes happens is that the director and actors come across a difficult bit to stage or to act and instead of continuing to dig deeper to overcome it, they ask the playwright to change the words to accommodate this impasse. Even when the playwright agrees to this, it sometimes takes them weeks to change even the simplest sentence. To change a "the" to an "and". At first, we may think this is pretentious or part of a power play on the part of the playwright, but after we read and stage play after play after play, we come the realize that the script is actually this beautiful intricate machine. I like to imagine it as this massive unbelievably complex kind of Antikythera[1] mechanism with many interlocking moving cogs, levers and dials. Like changing a word in the script, if even the smallest cog or lever is changed or replaced, the mechanism will not work as it did before and may stop working altogether. I imagine it as even an order of magnitude more complex than this as the machine also changes over time (the length of the performance) with groups of cogs and levers sliding out of the way and others taking their place only to slide back into place before the end. There is an elegance and fluidity to this choreography of complexity that is easily destroyed if changed.

To continue with this metaphor, the machine is not the story of the script; the story is whatever the dials are displaying moment by moment. In the traditional *Form vs Content* metaphor, this would be the content. What is the machine behind the dials? That is the way that story is being told. The form of the story. The same story can be told in many ways by

DOI: 10.4324/9781003223160-4

using different kinds of mechanisms behind the dials. There are many different forms to communicate the same content. The underlying role of sound design, or indeed any other production element in a show, is to help tell the story. Clearly, the story can still be effectively told with just actors on a bare stage without any of these complex production elements.

I witnessed this myself in 1988. I was on the Royal National Theatre's (RNT) world tour of Sir Peter Hall's production of *The Late Shakespeares – Cymbeline, The Winter's Tale* and *The Tempest*. After a stint in Moscow, we were due to play next at the Tbilisi Opera House in Soviet Georgia. To cut a long and interesting story short, the company flew to Tbilisi but our trucks with sets, lights, costumes, wigs and makeup and sound/music never arrived. Eventually, the actors and musicians had to perform in their everyday clothes with some borrowed items on an essentially bare stage. These were some of the most electrifying performances. Everyone agreed that without the gorgeous production elements that they were used to, the cast just acted their socks off instead. Now... we are talking about some very good actors, Sir Tim Pigott-Smith and Sir Michael Bryant (both sadly passed), Geraldine James, Shirley Henderson etc. The point is that the story still got told, but just using the mechanism of the script without the added mechanism of our production elements. In case you are wondering what happened to our trucks. They hightailed it out of the Soviet Union through Yugoslavia (as it was called then). Apparently, halfway down to Tbilisi their fuel was spiked, and they had to rebuild their carburetors in the middle of a desolate military highway. We were told after the fact that apparently the Russians did not want the Georgians to see *their* show! It's hard to know if that is true or not, but it does make for an interesting *Crime on the Orient Express* kind of story.

This difference between the story and the way it is being told is the reason that I have had a lot of difficulty teaching sound design using traditional methods of script analysis. It turns out that even if the students understand and master a particular method of script analysis (and some of the methods are truly insightful), I have found that it doesn't seem to actually help the student design sound for a play. At best, it provides an after-the-fact justification for what they wanted to do in the first place. Time after time, having completed the script analysis, the students would still choose their original pre-analysis sound cues. Most of these published methods of script analysis are really meant for actors and directors to find character motivation or changes in tension between characters over time. The job of theatre design is not to muscle-in on the acting and steal out from under their feet what the actors are already contributing. That is probably why these methods of script analysis are of little use for making creative design decisions. We designers *help tell the story that the actors are acting out*. These are two different things, but they are not often taught as such.

Over the years, I have developed and perfected my own unique way of analyzing how the story is being told. I have developed it into a whole process for designing sound and composing music that keeps it in the agile low effort realm of words until the last possible moments when it must become sound. I freely admit that in the early days, I was not aware I was doing this. I found that as I became more proficient at sound design, I wanted to include more sound ideas in the shows that I was designing, and I needed a way to organize and keep track of the huge amount of information. When our creativity is firing on all cylinders it is easy to lose track of things and tie ourselves in knots.

Figure 4.1 is an example from the 1994 production of *The Revengers' Comedies* by Alan Ayckbourn that was staged in the old Fichandler Theatre at Arena Stage directed by Doug Wager. This example is just one page of my provisional design ideas for every moment in the show. As well as being a playwright and director, Ayckbourn also ran his own theatre in the UK, so he has intimate knowledge of the technical and production side. He seems to always choose one production element to play around with in each of the plays he writes. In *A Chorus of Disapproval*, it was lighting. In *Revengers'*, the comedy is in using sounds that stand in for things that directly interact with the characters. It was a wonderful opportunity for sound which garnered Arena Stage a Helen Hayes nomination for the sound design.

Three decades ago, my design process had not fully coalesced into what I practice today; the process I outline in this book. However, I have always been excited about reading scripts for the shows I work on. The first reason is that I totally believe in the script and accept it as it is. I get lost in it as I would do any good book. I am by nature a skeptical person, but I do not judge scripts at all. I have no idea why this should be, but I am thankful for it as it really has helped in my journey developing a more resilient and reproducible process. I accept that the words, story and character are who they are and that my job is to identify the places in the script that excite me as a sound designer where I can practice my craft. Not just the sound cues in the stage directions but other places too where I think sound can make a difference or be fun to explore. I would then list everything and expand on each, imaginatively exploring them in an almost childlike way. What if this? What of that? I really wasn't aware at the time that it was a design process so much as it was the way

24 Script as Machine

Revengers' Comedies - Provisional Sound Design

   2. o Furtherfield House doorbell from drawing room. distant as if at the other end of the building
      1 o Doorbell straight but distant perspective
3. o Page 69. Scene change
   1 o Lights down on scene
      1. o Scene change music
         1 o Switched on Bach 2000 Cut #9
      2. o Office atmosphere fades up
         1 0 Fax machines
         2. o Telex
         3 o duplicators
         4 a pnnters
         5 0 phones
         6 o Typewnters
         7 o Desk Top clock bcking slightly fast
6. o Scene 5 (p89-p74). 4:15pm. Bruce Tick's offices at Lembridge Tennit.
   f. o Page 69. Scene change complete
      1 o Lights up on scene
         1. 0 Scene change music ends
         2. o Office atmosphere fades into scene revealing -
         3. o Slow typing which slightly lags behind the fade
            1 o Electnc typewriter has rtant
   2. O Page 73. Tests Walkman
      1 o She produces her cassette recorder She finds a pre-recorded cassette in her bag She loads the machine and tests rt
         1 . o A short burst of fai y funky pop music
            1 0 ?
   3. o Page 74. Karen starts her walkman
      1 o The phone at the other end starts to ring She starts up her cassette machine and lets it play near the mouthpiece.
         1. o Funky Pop Cassette
            1 0 ?
   " · o Page 74. Karen stops her walkman
      1 O She nngs off and SWltches off the cassette player
   5. o Page 74. Scene change
      1 O Lights down on scene
         1. o Office atmosphere swells briefly
            1 0 Fax machines
            2 o Telex
            3 0 duplicators
            4 o pnnters
            5 0 phones
            6 o Typewnters
            7 o Desk Top clock ticking slightly fast
         2. o Scene cahange music
            1 o Switched on Bach 2000 Cut #10
         3. o Office atmosphere cross fades into Piggery atmosphere
            1 o Lots of piggrunts
            2 a Pig squeels
            3 O Bucketsounds
            4 0 slopping sounds
7. o Scene 6 (p74-p79). 11:00am. The Piggery at the Saxton-Bl/1/ngs' farm.
   f . o Page 74. Scenbe change complete
      1 O I.jghts up on scene Scene change music ends revealing the piggery at the Saxton-Billings' farm. A lot of appropnate sounds as ..
         1. o Scene change music ends
         2. O Piggery atmosphere - Runs throughout scene
         3. a Specific pig sounds to be used as directed
   2. o Page 77. Gunshot
      1 0 Henry ".. lets have less of that please"
         1 o A distant gunshot from outside
            1 o 12 Bore gunshot
   3. o Page 77. Gunshot
      1 o Henry "Would he?"
         1. o Another distant gunshot
            1 o 12 bore gunshot
   4. o Page 78. Gunshots
      1 o Imogen . " . I think she's rather beautifur'
         1. o Two closer gunshots in quick succession
            1 0 Both barrels of 12 bore gunshots
   5. o Page 78. Gunshot
      1 O Henry·. That will keep me going for-oh hours "
         1. o Another Closer gunshot
            1 0 12 bore gunshot
   6. o Page 79. Voice off stage
      1 o Imogen "Where's Clem? Can't Clem do 1!?"
         1 0 Anthony's voice off stage

Fig 4.1. Page 6 of my provisional sound design for *The Revengers' Comedies*. (A list of sound cues including their subitems.)

I enjoyed designing the sound for drama. Probably a similar feeling that you the reader have.

In those days, I used a PC program called EccoPro (sadly now abandoned), which had the ability to organize and display multiple views of the same information in different ways. In today's software parlance, we would think of this as a kind of tagging and filtering. This ability influenced the way I developed my process of prototyping using words. For example, Figure 4.1 is one page of seventeen pages of my sequential list or *view* of sound cues from curtain-up music to curtain call. Using my process, I can bring each sound cue with its subitems into another list or *view* and sequence it in a different way while still keeping all the subitems belonging to the sound cue. For example, an additional *view* could be a list of the sound cues of the different locations in the story, Bruce Tick's office at Lembridge Tennit, the piggery at the Saxton-Billing's farm, the Gymkhana, the Albert Bridge SW3 etc. Using different views to group together the sound effects that built the various different locations in the play allowed me to make sure that all the sound cues used in those specific locations all sounded similar and from the same place.

In yet another view, I could bring in all the cues I needed to record. With traditional tagging, I can assemble a view with a list of everything that is tagged with the same tag, but it would be sequenced one after the other in the same order as in the original view it was created in. The sound cue on page six of the script would be after the sound cue with the same tag on page four. In the prototyping system I developed, I could rearrange the order of these in every view without it rearranging the order in the original view (or any of the other views). This allowed me to rearrange the list of my recordings to fit in with the availability of the actors and was not dependent on where that dialogue occurred in the script. It also was not dependent on the order it occurred in my original provisional sound design view or any other view. Sadly, I don't have an example of this from *Revengers'* to show the reader as I lost a lot of my physical archive over one summer recess when my university office got infested with mold.

The prototyping process using words that I was developing had some other features that made it useful for organizing my sound designs. For this, I am going to use the widely understood *parent/child* relationship used in lists. Any *child* subitem could be tagged and brought into another view and it would bring the *parent* items with it. For instance, I could tag all the typewriter subitems and bring them into a typewriter view and I could see which parent sound cues they were associated with. For example, this allowed me to see that many of the cues were typewriters from the same office, but a couple were from a sweet shop (candy store)[2] so, this informed me that I would need to find two different sounding typewriters.

The final part of my prototyping process using words was the most powerful. If I looked at my list of typewriters in the typewriter view, I could rewrite their description or add new *child* subitems. For instance, maybe I wanted some of the typewriters to have a return carriage bell to add to the perceived efficiency of the office and for the other typewriter in the sweet shop, I would not need it. These changes would propagate back and be reflected in the original provisional sound design view. This allowed me to check that any refinement I had made while working in the specific typewriters view would also work in the cue sequence view with all the other sound cues around them. For instance, if the sweetshop had an over-the-door shopkeeper's bell[3] that would tinkle every time the door opened or closed, I would not add a typewriter carriage return bell to that typewriter sound as they would sound too similar and it could be confusing to an audience and, therefore, ultimately distracting[4]. I would then know that I would have to find another way to communicate either efficiency or inefficiency without using a return carriage bell. Maybe hesitant pecking at the keys for example?

It is human nature to be overly expansive and vague in our aspirations and desires but using this prototyping process using words provided a structure and ability for me as a designer to counter this. It allowed me to drill down deeper and deeper, figuring out what it was *exactly* that I wanted. It also allowed me to organize and inspect this detailed information in many unique ways and develop my ability to manipulate it and further refine my choices.

Little did I know at the time of designing *The Revengers' Comedies* that I was building my own intricate machine like that of the script for keeping design in the agile world of words; that I was developing a process that we could totally understand and freely adapt. A process that we could retreat into, that consistently produced results. A process that is easy to practice even when the *muse* is not close to us on that day or with that particular play or production. That I was developing a resilient process that would give results time after time. That I was developing a new form of prototyping.

Notes

1 Ancient corroded unknown complex mechanism artifact from Greece.
2 There is no sweet shop in *The Revengers' Comedies*. This is just an example I have made up.

3 Traditionally, shopkeeper bells were used to alert the shopkeepers who lived in the back of their premises that someone had entered their store.
4 Because the audience would have to break their suspension of disbelief and take time to try and figure it out.

References

Ayckbourn, Alan. (1994). *The Revengers' Comedies*. Directed by Doug Wager, Washington, DC: Arena Stage, Fichandler Theatre.

Polash, P. & Perez, B. (1993). *EccoPro (V1)* [Computer Software]. Belleview, WA: Arabesque Software.

Shakespeare, William. (1988). *The Late Shakespeares – Cymbeline, the Winter's Tale and the Tempest*. Directed by Sir Peter Hall, World Tour. London, UK: Royal National Theatre.

Symbols, Narrative and Vocabulary   5

So, why couldn't the shopkeeper's bell in the previous chapter be used as well as the return carriage bell of the typewriter? The short answer is that they sound too much like each other and yet we want the audience to quickly *learn* that they symbolize two completely different things in our show; someone entering a sweet shop verses the efficiency of an office. Let's explore this in more depth as it has a direct bearing on what I add as sub-items to my lists when using my prototyping process using words

There is a whole area of study called *Semiotics* that deals with this, but without getting into the weeds… Symbols are split into the *signifier* (a material thing), in our case, the unique sound of the shopkeeper's bell, and what it *signifies* (the concept it refers to) that the door to a small shop is being opened or closed and that someone is entering or exiting the store. You will notice that we have one signifier, but we already have three things being signified: a door, a small shop and someone entering.

Both the *signifier* and the *signified* are distinguished by what they are *not* as opposed to what they are. For instance, the shopkeeper's bell is not the sound of a church bell (and any myriad of other bells) and it doesn't mean it is Sunday (or any other day). Both a church bell and the shopkeeper's bell sound very different and clearly symbolize two very different things. One is not the other and vice versa. Now that we understand this, we realize that the *ding* of the typewriter carriage return bell can easily be mistaken for one of the individual *dings* that make up the *tinkling* of a shopkeeper's bell. We cannot now say that one is clearly *not* the other and vice versa. They are both too close in sound and not distinct enough from each other for the symbol to be quickly and easily comprehended. This is

DOI: 10.4324/9781003223160-5

especially true today when we can go years in our everyday lives without hearing either the tinkle of a shopkeeper's bell or a return carriage bell of a typewriter. If an audience has already *learned* the shopkeeper's bell, then the single *ding* of the carriage return bell could be mistaken for an initial hesitant push of the sweetshop door before opening it fully. As a young boy, I didn't have the strength to easily open the heavily sprung door of a sweetshop without giving it a really good shove. My initial attempt usually just produced one ding instead of a full tinkling of the shopkeeper's bell.

What seems to happen in this situation is that an audience's first understanding of a symbol seems to be applied to subsequent uses of similar sounds unless they are obviously different. It is as if that first use of the sound has *hijacked* that symbolic meaning for both its subsequent uses as well as other similar sounds.

The signifier and the signified being distinguished by what they are *not* rather than what they are actually helps us as designers. For instance, it means that we can find or make many different sounds of different church bells and an audience will still understand them as church bells and that it is Sunday. In fact, we could make a soundscape of a whole city of churches ringing their bells on a Sunday and each bell would be different and represent a different church and the whole cacophony would be immediately understandable to an audience as various churches ringing their church bells on a Sunday as long as they understood that first bell as a church bell.

The signifier and signified are conspicuous in all areas of design. Take for example a costume design for the opening scenes for *Romeo and Juliet* by William Shakespeare. Until we know who ROMEO is and who TYBALT is, we need to dress the two rival families noticeably differently otherwise an audience will get confused. No matter what the costume, an experienced costume designer will make sure their costumes will also communicate family affiliation and relative status within that family, at least for the start of the play while the audience is still learning who is who. For instance, although being a member of the Montague family, ROMEO sometimes acts differently to the other family members. So, a costume designer may choose to change the *family affiliation-ness* of their costume design slightly by swapping out, adding or removing an element of ROMEO's costume communicating his status and uniqueness while still firmly placing him in the rival Montague family. They change the signifier slightly so that they still signify family but also now signify a sense of separateness.

As with costumes, a simple sound cue can communicate far more than we would think. To demonstrate this, I usually play to my sound students the sound of a typical household *ding-dong* doorbell sourced from the internet that neither I nor they have ever heard before (a double-blind experiment). I then ask them to describe the type of house the doorbell is from. How many bedrooms? Garden? Grounds? Pets? Metropolitan? Suburban? Rural? Elderly? Young? Children? Country? Season? Time of day? Who is at the door? Good? Evil? Anticipated? Random? Friend? Foe? Stranger?... I find it amazing how much agreement there is amongst the students in their answers. They even agree if the house has a swimming pool or not. Even simple sound effects have so much unintentional symbolic *baggage* associated with them.

Some of this associated baggage are signifiers as we have already discussed but a typical household *ding-dong* doorbell also has all these other *connotations* burbling under the surface. Whereas symbol's signifiers and signified are about what is material and the concepts they embody, symbols can also mean something. They have a literal meaning which is called their *denotation* and have secondary and cultural meanings, which are called their *connotations*.

Like me, at this point, you are probably getting a little confused. Since we are not researching this subject, we don't really need to know the correct subclassifications of symbols. What we do need to accept is that it happens. Audiences read into our design choices all these other secondary concepts and meanings. So, to recap using our simple *Ding-Dong* doorbell sound; a *signifier* is the doorbell sound, it *signifies* someone arriving at the door and wanting to be let in, but the sound also *denotes* a suburban house and encapsulates *connotations* about the culture and who is at the door. This explanation is overly simplistic for what is a very complicated subject. But the point is that as well as a particular design choice generating all this baggage, we designers can also work backward and choose what baggage we would like our design choice to represent and then design something that fulfills that. As I continued developing my prototyping process using words for my designs, I started populating its *parent/child* lists with more and more of this baggage that I wanted each sound effect to elicit in an audience.

The ability to tag and filter and arrange these *parent/child* entries into different views allowed me to make sure that not only did the sound cue work together sequentially as the show progressed as a *Narrative* progressing from the first cue through to the last cue, but that they also made sense when assembled in groups of similar sounding cues. I call these groups *Vocabularies*. In our early days when we start designing sound, sometimes our choice of sound cue responds adequately to the specific moment in the show, but all the cues don't seem to hang together as an identifiable whole. Someone would never say "Oh! That sounds like a cue from such-and-such a show". This is a very subtle distinction but the easiest way to understand this is to think of the music that John Williams composed for all the Star Wars movies.

John Williams' compositions span 42 years and yet they all sound like they are from the Star Wars saga. Not only does his music respond to the specific moment in each movie where it occurs, but it also subtly mimics the rise and fall of different emotional elements within the saga. One such is the force that the Skywalker family possesses. Compare the music for Luke Skywalker with that of Anakin his predecessor. Although Williams uses similar themes, he also uses fragmentation, development and orchestration to accomplish this rise and demise and rise again of this supernatural element. Also remember, Williams did not start at the beginning of the saga and develop his musical ideas from there. He started in the middle and had to give his musical ideas a past to develop from and a future to develop into. He constructed an identifiable vocabulary to draw from so that the connotation was never diluted even though it changed over this rise and fall. It all sounded like the music from Star Wars even though it was made up of very different music composed decades apart.

Sound is the youngest of the traditional four[1] major design specializations in theatre and is still in the process of maturing. If we look at the others, they are already choosing or developing a limited pallet—a specific vocabulary—as an identifiable characteristic of their design for each show. The colors, textures and shapes of the scenic elements are usually from a purposefully limited pallet. The fabrics, colors and textures of the costumes are from a limited pallet of fabrics and drapes. Also, the lighting is built around a purposefully chosen limited group of colors (gels) and gobos. With these other specializations, we can take a piece of scenery or a costume or a photo of a lit scene out of the context of the show and we can usually identify that it was from a particular show because it looks like it was from that show. Sadly sometimes, this cannot be said for sound. Sometimes our sound cues just sound like a collection of misfits.

These two different ways of looking at a sound design, the narrative with its sound cues in the order that they would be heard in a show and also the individual vocabularies with its groups of similar cues, allowed me to develop a more resilient and deeper process for designing sound

32 Symbols, Narrative and Vocabulary

than I was practicing up until that point. I would constantly hop between refining the cue using the narrative and refining the same cue using the vocabulary. I would adjust the words in one view so that they fit into the context of the other cues around it. I would then see how that adjustment looked in the other view. If needed, I would adjust some more until they made sense in that other view with the cues around it. I would do this until they fit both views simultaneously. It would only be after all that prototyping and winnowing with words had been accomplished and a stable product arrived upon that I would feel I now had a credible design idea.

There was a formative book from the late seventies by Douglas Hofstadter called *Gödel, Escher, Bach: An Eternal Golden Braid*. I was captivated by the book cover and illustrations which also alluded to the playfully written, though dense, thesis inside. The illustration (Figure 5.1) depicted an object that casts a shadow of a different letter depending on where the light was shining from. Like my resulting credible design and provisional sound cue, the vocabulary and narrative were the shadows cast in the different axes by a central essence. For my provisional sound cue to rise to that of a *central essence*, it must cast a perfect shadow in the narrative as well as the vocabulary for me to feel that it had become credible.

Ah! But what about the third shadow in the GEB image below? Well, if we think about it, two of the shadows, the vocabulary and narrative,

Fig 5.1. GEB triplet casting its three orthogonal shadows. Photo curtesy of Douglas R. Hofstadter. (Diagram showing suspended object casting three shadows on three different surfaces.)

are derived from the script. The third light source that needs to also cast a perfect shadow is the direction that the specific production is taking—the overall creative concept that is emerging from collaborating with the director and the other designers. The *central essence* of the provisional sound cue must also cast a perfect shadow when illuminated by this additional source. That doesn't necessarily require another view in my document; it is more like a continuing conversation with the director and other designers. We are constantly seeing what shadow the sound cue is casting in this third plane and then adjusting the cue further to cast a perfect shadow without disrupting the other two shadows. This shadows being cast visualization of the concept of prototyping using words is a bit ephemeral but then again so is sound.

Once we start viewing our sound cues from the sequential perspective as a narrative, and also from the grouped perspective of vocabularies, we realize that like the script the individual groups of sound cues—the vocabularies—also make a journey. Or at least they should. The journey the sound cues make in the narrative is easy to understand as they mimic the journey of the script, but each vocabulary (the list of similar sound cues) needs to also have its own journey. That is essentially what the composer John Williams did with the music representing the force in the Skywalker family. His music for the force made a journey in and of itself mimicking the rise and fall and rise again of that power: a journey different than the sequence of when the movies were released.

The essence of design is planning and intention, *designing* a course of action to reach a goal, not simply forging ahead and later pretending intention (as I had discovered using traditional character-centric script analysis). Rather than just seeing what journey each of our vocabularies make, we can decide in advance what journey they should make to help tell the story more effectively. For instance, continuing the example of the typewriter from *The Revengers' Comedies* earlier (Ayckbourne, 2015); as his grasp on power and his control erodes throughout the show for the bloated character of the office executive BRUCE TICK, maybe the typing should stop and start more often, and should falter more with indecision as the play progresses. Maybe there should be decreasing carriage return bells per minute to infer less efficiency? If we as a designer decide to do this, we can easily make it happen. The hard bit is focusing on it in the first place and making it intentional. That is what is achieved by specifying in the view the journey each vocabulary needs to take. Having decided a vocabularies' journey we can adjust each cue in that vocabulary to reflect that journey.

As a key practice in this approach, once I have my various vocabularies of similar sound cues, at the top of that vocabulary I write a small paragraph describing that vocabulary and the journey I want it to take. I then adjust each cue so that it conforms to that journey. Since this journey paragraph is now the *parent* of the *children* sound cues in this specific vocabulary, we will be able to see it when looking at that same sound cue in the narrative view. Every time a cue from that vocabulary appears in the narrative, it will have picked up our overall journey description. We can now see if the updated cues also still work in sequence in our narrative. Does that journey still make sense where that cue appears as the story unfolds? If not, we further adjust the cues and then once again go back to the vocabulary view and see if those adjustments (that have now propagated back to that view) still conform to our designed journey for that specific vocabulary. If they still do not, we do have the option of updating the journey that the vocabulary should take to make it fit the newly updated cue. Both cues and journeys get adjusted so that it eventually works in both views. All these changes are so fast and easy because we are still in our prototyping material/medium of words. Imagine how much time and effort it would take doing this process building and changing sounds instead of words?

Once I have made these changes, I may find that other sound cues and their corresponding vocabularies also now need adjusting to fit these newly adjusted sound cues in the narrative. Maybe the sound of the road work outside the office should become a little more manic to reflect the internal dissolution of the office over time? This would be manipulating a connotation of one sound cue as a proxy, or associative, connotation of another sound cue[2]. So once again, I go back to the existing "exterior sounds" vocabulary and rewrite the journey paragraph to reflect this change. I then adjust the sound cues in that vocabulary to reflect this new journey that now mimics the demise of the office power structure. Then back to the narrative to see how they have propagated back and if they still make sense or need further adjustment.

Fortunately, this is much easier to do than to write about, so I apologize if my explanation hasn't made it easy to grasp. To use the *Gödel, Escher, Bach* trip-let image from earlier. Supposing we started off with a solid wooden cube that was casting rectangular shadows in the three directions. We could start chipping away at one side and start to cast the shadow of a G instead of a rectangle. We would then need to start chipping away at another side to cast the shadow of E. We would probably have to chip away at both sides at the same time to make sure what we were doing on one side of the cube to cast a better shadow of a G was not compromising the casting of the E shadow and vice versa. The Narrative view and the Vocabulary view equate to the two different sides of the cube we are working on, and we must constantly chip away at each side to cast the perfect shadow that we are desiring. But realize... we are chipping away at only one single cube. Similarly, using the two views of the Narrative and the Vocabulary, we are working on only one single written sound effect. When the sound effect is perfect it will be perfect in the Narrative view as well as the Vocabulary view. We use one to check the other and we use both to check whether our design for that cue is completed.

Notes

1 Four in the sense of being listed on the title page of theatre program or playbill.
2 This is no different from using the sound of thunder to imply impending doom for a character or situation.

References

Ayckbourn, A. (2015). *The Revengers' Comedies*. New York, NY: Samuel French.
Hofstadter, Douglas R. (1979). *Gödel, Escher, Bach: An Eternal Golden Braid*. New York, NY: Basic Books.
Polash, P. & Perez, B. (1993). *EccoPro (V1)* [Computer Software]. Belleview, WA: Arabesque Software.
Shakespeare, William. (1974). Romeo and Juliet. In *The Riverside Shakespeare*, edited by G. Blakemore Evans et al., vol. 2. Boston, MA: Houghton Mifflin.
Williams, John. (2016). *Star Wars — The Ultimate Soundtrack Collection: The Original Soundtrack from the Motion Pictures*. Los Angeles, CA: Sony Masterworks.

Granularization 6

Realize at this point that I am building my sound cues from its constituent parts rather than just pulling them in as a complete recorded sound cue from a sound effect library. If we go back to the description of the process IDEO used. The post-it notes on the wall allow the short description to be moved and rearranged without losing track of them, but since they also only encapsulate one of many single ideas that may end up in the eventual design, they define the smallest level of granularity that can be manipulated. We must conceptually carve out a piece of the world and separate it from the rest before we can move it independently of everything else around it. This level of *granularity* that we operate on is a personal decision we make about ourselves as a designer. Since I really enjoy designing sound, and since we cannot design within something that is already fixed and inseparable, I always take things apart right down to their elemental nuts and bolts and reassemble them in the way I want. This purposeful choice of level of granularity is consistent across all design fields. For instance, I have had the honor of working with costume designers who work down to the level of individual sequins and feathers! Now that we have cleaved apart and exposed these minute variables, we designers can now make choices about how we want to reassemble them or vary them to achieve the *look* or the sound at that specific moment in the show.

This choice of my personal level of granularity stems out of two experiences from my career. The first is that I realized early on that pulling props and set pieces from a warehouse and pulling costumes from a costume collection did not look the same on the stage as when those

DOI: 10.4324/9781003223160-6

elements were designed and built from scratch for that specific production or for that actor. At the RNT where I started my career, we prided ourselves at the time that everything (except shoes) was built in-house. Wigs were ventilated (knotted), fabrics were dyed, we even had one of the few remaining armories left in London that could build whole suits of armor. When pulling and using an item from storage, the item defines the level of granularity. When designing and constructing that item from scratch, that level of granularity and manipulation is so much finer, and its *fit* into a production ends up being more snug. How a design element hugs a production is perceivable… if you look for it. This level of granularity obviously requires many more choices and decisions, so as a designer we better be up to it.

The second experience was when sound effects started to be released on CDs. Being the sound nerd that I am, I would listen to every new SFX CD in my car on the way to and from work. I experienced all these different sounds without reading their track titles and without knowing what most of them were recordings of. I only cared about what I imagined they sounded like; what they symbolized; what an audience would hear them as. As every sound effect on the CD was made up of many sound elements within each recording, I could disentangle them in my mind and assess each of them separately. I would realize that the scraping sound sounded like what I imagine a portcullis closing would sound like and the rustle of the fabric sounded like a wind on a desolate frozen icefield. Without realizing it, I was training myself to take apart sounds and figure out what each part of them could symbolize (or didn't as the case may be). I became aware that inside many sound recordings were nuggets that had very powerful symbology and many other parts that were just filler—an indeterminate bed that did not actually sound like any particular thing.

I would rip these CDs onto a hard disk and make a note of the names of the tracks that had the interesting symbolic sounds so I could find them later. Although these names on the sound files when ripped were descriptive, they didn't describe what I found interesting which is why I made my own notes. Now, when designing sound effects, I start out by building them as a group of these nuggets, these sound symbols described in words, but I also know where I can find each actual sound that corresponds to that symbol without having to include any of that needless filler.

Often, the term essence is sometimes misused. I mean that a mixture of sounds, containing both "essential" and "non-essential" components cannot, itself, be considered essential. Rather, I purposefully choose a level of granularity that allows me to break the sound apart, separating elements with specific symbolism from the mix and reconstruct the cue defining in words only the truly *essential* sounds I need. The result is that I am not locked into a specific sounding cue, but rather I am dealing with a concept or idea for a sound; a conceptual essence which I prototype and describe using words. This allows me to make changes at any point in the tech or design process since my understanding of the cue is not about a specific sound, but a symbolic essence of a cue that fulfills the specific need in the script and that also delights the audience. As a conceptual essence and not a specific sound, I can see that this specific intention could be achieved in more than one way using many different options.

Maybe this conceptual essence would be more easily understood as an example. In the production of *Dracula* in 2004 adapted and directed by Preston Lane at Triad Stage, we wanted to button the last moment of the show with a shiver down the audiences' spine. We all knew as a conceptual essence what we were wanting to achieve but it was hard for us to deliver it using either sound or music. It had to be short as it just lasted a split-second and at that point, we had just ended a hymn being sung by the characters. Having diegetic music followed immediately by non-diegetic music would potentially confuse an audience at a point where we really needed them there with us. I eventually suggested to the director that the conceptual essence could be achieved by the angelic choirboy biting the head off a rat. And that is what we did. Alone in the spotlight having finished angelically singing his hymn he bit the head of an edible rat provided by props with edible blood running down his angelic little cheeks. The audience loved it. They collectively shivered! Dracula was not dead after all! Because it was developed as a conceptual essence of a sound cue it was easy to find other ways of achieving it when sound design couldn't.

As I said in the last chapter, design is about intention and not after-the-fact justification. Designing cues as granular conceptual essences is just specifying in detail how you want an audience to react; to feel and what you want them to understand. Yes, we can use sound to do it, but we needn't. This is the ultimate adaptability, to specify at such a granular level that the intention can be fulfilled by any of the production values—not just sound. The enabling of this level of adaptability will be discussed more in the second part of the book when we discuss the design implementation process from designer run onwards.

The sound design I created for a production of *Picnic* by William Inge provides a good illustration of the flexibility enabled by this granular level of design. In the story, various characters are known to be arriving or leaving by the characteristic sound each of their pickup trucks make. We obviously never see the trucks. The sound of trucks arriving, and then characters entering, or the characters exiting and the sound of the trucks departing are all out of view off-stage from a vom or exit. For our production, the set designer Howard Jones laid the stage with real turf. Of course, it all had died by the first preview but that was the point. It was meant to look like Kansas in the height of summer. This dead grass extended beyond a white picket fence of the set and into the off-stage vom where the truck sound cues came from. So, I originally built the sounds of the trucks arriving with the sound of their individual tires on hard compacted turf

I have found over my career that set designers come in two flavors, *architectural* or *textural*. With the architectural designers, the set we get at the start of tech is the set that we see on opening night with very little added. With the textural designers, the set is continually dressed, texture upon texture, doodad upon doodad, throughout the tech process and arrives at opening night quite different from when it initially went in. Jones is the second kind and one day I arrived in the theatre only to find that the dead grass in front of the picket fence leading to the vom now had gravel over it indicating a gravel track to the house. I had to scramble, but because I build all my cues from individual granular elements, It was easy to remove the sound of turf and replace it with the sound of tires on gravel under all the wheels of the different trucks so as to fit in and still give a sense of the different horsepower (weight) of each truck. As a coda to this story, when the turf dried up and died, all the bugs left the dirt and stayed in the theatre throughout the run. It truly was a recreation of Kansas in the height of summer. Audiences occasionally swatted themselves as they watched the show!

Of course, all this hopping between vocabulary and narrative only works if what is changed in one view is automatically updated in the other view so that it remains the same. With the sad demise of EccoPro and the fact that I now work on a Mac, I have had to do it all manually, updating each view myself to make sure that my prototype using words is the same in each view but just arranged differently. However, the good news is that I have recently discovered a way to do this again automatically using Microsoft Word for Mac. A detailed description of this method can be found using the following link on the publisher's website[1].

The examples used in the linked description on the publisher's website are necessarily very simple sound cues because I want to focus on demonstrating how to achieve this concept of the same information appearing in two or more different views organized in different ways. In reality, sound cues are a lot more detailed and nuanced than this. Please feel free to experiment with other software to accomplish this. If you find something that works, let me know and I will update the linked document. In the following chapter, I will share with you how this level of detail and nuance helps a designer to not only serve the playwright's intention but also engage with an audience.

Note

1 http://www.routledge.com/9781032121185.

References

Inge, William. (2009). *Picnic*. Directed by Preston Lane. Greensboro, NC: Triad Stage, The Pearl Theatre.

Polash, P. & Perez, B. (1993). *EccoPro (V1)* [Computer Software]. Belleview, WA: Arabesque Software.

Stoker, Bram. (2004). *Dracula*. Adapted and Directed by Preston Lane. Greensboro, NC: Triad Stage, The Pearl Theatre.

7

Purpose, Meaning, Reason and Research

Cues get cut because whatever it was that they originally contributed to in the telling of the story at that specific point in the script is now no longer needed. They also get cut because the actor or some other production element (sets, lighting, costumes, projections) is now making that contribution instead, or because of redundancy when there are too many design elements all making the same contribution. Directors are usually the person doing the cutting of cues. They are constantly assessing if the tech time needed to achieve something is worth it or not. Maybe that specific contribution can be completely done without and not impact the story. Maybe an actor moving in a different way can more easily achieve the same effect with much less effort and loss of tech time. Cues almost never get cut because they are not malevolent enough or comedic enough. In cases like that, they just get changed not cut. What gets cut are cues that don't have a valid storytelling *purpose* anymore. So, it is important to understand in intricate detail the purpose of every cue.

Let's use an example from a real show *A Streetcar Named Desire* by Tennessee Williams. At one point in the show, STANLEY returns to his apartment unnoticed during the day and overhears his visiting sister-in-law BLANCHE telling his wife STELLA that he is a brutish thug, and that STELLA should leave him. Below is the section from the script.

> *[Outside, a train approaches. They are silent till the noise subsides. They are both in the bedroom. Under cover of the train's noise Stanley enters from outside. He stands unseen by the women,*

DOI: 10.4324/9781003223160-7

> *holding some packages in his arms, and overhears their following conversation. He wears an undershirt and grease-stained seersucker pants.]*
>
> BLANCHE: Well—if you'll forgive me—he's common!
> STELLA: Why, yes, I suppose he is.
> BLANCHE: Suppose! You can't have forgotten that much of our bringing up, Stella, that you just suppose that any part of a gentleman's in his nature! Not one particle, no! Oh, if he was just—ordinary! Just plain—but good and wholesome, but—no. There's something downright—bestial—about him! You're hating me saying this, aren't you?
> STELLA [coldly]: Go on and say it all, Blanche.
> BLANCHE: He acts like an animal, has an animal's habits....

The purpose of the sound cue of the train approaching is obvious. It allows the audience to believe that STANLEY has entered his apartment *unheard by the other characters*. This has allowed him to overhear a conversation that was not meant for his ears. This conversation introduces a tension between BLANCHE and STANLEY that in part drives the rest of the play. It also introduces tension in the audience who now know something that the characters BLANCHE and STELLA do not know. This alters our interpretation of anything that STANLEY does or anything he says to STELLA and to BLANCHE for the rest of the play. This moment is very important. Its purpose is so important that it would be very hard to cut this train approaching sound cue. It is hard to imagine its purpose being provided by re-blocking the scene or by another production element, though not impossible… STANLEY could overtly tiptoe in unheard in a symbolically mimed *silent comedic entrance*. BLANCH and STELLA could cover their ears at that moment for some inextricable reason. A projection of a train passing over the set would also be understood by an audience in a synesthetic kind of way to stand in for the blanketing sound of a train passing. But these changes would be hard for an audience to accept unless the ground for them had been prepared earlier on. They would also have grave repercussions for the rest of the production. The collateral damage to the characters that these choices would leave would be hard to integrate into the rest of the story. The cue therefore has a purpose!

Purpose, Meaning, Reason and Research   43

Williams could have fulfilled this purpose in any number of ways. He could have had a New Orleans Jazz Band pass close by outside at that point. He could also have had cats knock over a bunch of metal trash cans outside. Both these different sounds would have covered STANLEY's entrance. Like me, you are probably thinking that neither of these substitutes would work even though they fulfill the purpose, and you would be correct. The reason is that sound cues also need to convey to an audience a specific feeling and have specific understandable meanings. These are the connotations and baggage we discussed in a previous chapter. Think of the meaning/feeling of a sound cue as the cues character. Like an actor, a sound cue can do something. That is the purpose, but the way the actor does it is the character they are playing. That is the sound cue's meaning/feeling.

Williams' choice of a train passing has a very specific connotation. First, it has already been set up by dialogue in an earlier scene…

> BLANCHE: … What are you doing in a place like this?
> STELLA: Now, Blanche—
> BLANCHE: Oh, I'm not going to be hypocritical, I'm going to be honestly critical about it! Never, never, never in my worst dreams could I picture—Only Poe! Only Mr. Edgar Allan Poe!—could do it justice! Out there I suppose is the ghoul-haunted woodland of Weir! [*She laughs.*]
> STELLA: No, honey, those are the L & N tracks.

Secondly, it reminds us that BLANCHE is out of her comfort zone and confirms in us her imperative desire to rescue STELLA. The brutish and overpowering sound of a passing freight train stands in for the brutish and overpowering world that STELLA has descended into. STANLEY using this brutish and overpowering sound to mask his entrance unnoticed implies that he can navigate successfully in this world because he is part of it, and it is part of him, brutish and overpowering. The passing New Orleans Jazz Band would have the connotation of Mardi Grass or a funeral procession. A meaning/feeling of a celebration and party that would not have helped tell this specific aspect of the story even though it would have masked the sound of STANLEY's entrance. As for the metal trash cans, even though the naughty cats have already been used on two previous occasions, each time their purpose was to steal the attention of the characters and make them stop what they were doing and look around them to figure out what is making the noise. This is the last thing that we want BLANCHE or STELLA to do as they will notice that STANLEY has entered and is eavesdropping on them.

There is also another reason that the trash cans would not work and that is simply because they are a sound that symbolizes a moment in time and STANLEY's entrance needs time to be accomplished. Even if we extended the cue using lots of metal trash cans falling like dominos and tacked on a tail of spinning metal lids, it may still not be long enough to fulfill the purpose of the cue. This is another issue we have when we are starting out designing sound, we sometimes try to use a momentary sound to cover something that is passing and takes time to unfold. Or the other way around, we inadvertently try to use a sound that takes time to unfold and be gone to cover what is just a momentary opportunity in the story.

Williams is such an expert builder of intricate mechanisms within his scripts. Look at the dialogue that immediately precedes the section where STANLEY enters.

> *[There is a pause.]*
> BLANCHE: May I—speak—plainly?
> STELLA: Yes, do. Go ahead. As plainly as you want to.
> *[Outside, a train approaches. They are silent till the noise subsides. They are both in the bedroom....*

BLANCHE has not made any headway at this point convincing STELLA to leave so she is forced to get personal about STANLEY and take the conversation to the next level. Just as Williams sets up this anticipation for the audience, he interrupts it with the train and prolongs the anticipation such that when STANLEY enters unnoticed the tension between BLANCHE and STELLA has been amplified. Obviously, the train approaches and will fade in quickly over those last few lines and stop the conversation, thereby keeping the audience on tenterhooks until it has passed. Williams is masterful!

There is also a third thing that every sound cue should have in our word-based prototype. As well as a purpose and a meaning/feeling (character), it also needs a justification. It also needs a reason there is a sound cue in the first place. It needs to be anchored in the script, in the dialogue or stage directions. Even if it is an opportunity for a sound cue that we want to create ourselves and not necessarily a specific need or stage direction from the script, it needs justification. I bring in every possible reference in the script that supports or helps define the sound cue. The small comments about it by the characters in previous or future scenes or pieces from other stage directions. I always bring these in verbatim quoting directly from the script and I always bring them in with page numbers so I can always reference back to them. It is surprising how many times I think one thing, and when I go back to the dialogue and stage directions, I realize it says something slightly different.

A good example of finding justification within the script for a totally new sound cue that has potential impact can be found at the end of *A Streetcar Named Desire*. In the scene change before the last scene, we have STANLEY and BLANCHE in the bedroom alone together for one of the few times during the show and we are led to believe that STANLEY rapes BLANCHE in the ensuing transition. In our production at Triad Stage in Greensboro, NC in October 2005, I convinced the director Preston Lane that the telephone should ring interrupting the action on stage. My justification was that previously when talking about his silk pajamas, STANLEY tells BLANCHE (and the audience) "When the telephone rings and they say, 'You've got a son!' I'll tear this off and wave it like a flag!" The anticipation is set up for a phone call symbolizing the delivery of their baby which under normal circumstances would be a happy family event. To have the telephone ring just as STANLEY pins BLANCHE to the bed and the lights go down on the scene for the ensuing ruination, not only heightens the incongruity of imminent fatherhood and rapist, but it also sets up a potential escape for BLANCHE.

Most audiences in regional theatre have probably seen *Streetcar* before and they all know that there is no escape for BLANCHE. But to have this tease put in front of them heightened the following horrifying descent into the scene change and unseen rape. Night after night, watching the audience lean forward in their seats in hope as the telephone rang. Watching STANLEY freeze and do a double take towards the telephone with obvious indecision before visibly deciding and continuing his attack, then made the audiences slam themselves back in their seats. Without being gratuitous and exposing more of the actual deed it heightened the unseen abomination. Theatrical catharsis in its purest form.

Lastly, where needed, I have a section for research if anything is mentioned that I need to know more about. I copy the relevant snippets from my research into that section along with a URL so I can go back and explore it further if I need to.

This puts all the information I need in this one place, so I don't have to hunt through the script or the research or anything. It is like a detective's whiteboard with all the evidence, photos and relationships displayed on it. Being all in one place and within view all the time, ideas can ruminate, connections can be made, and understanding can emerge. It all makes for quite a bulky amount of information for this *prototype-in-words* of each sound cue, but most word processing software can handle this by collapsing and expanding parent/child subsections to make it more manageable. In the next chapter, I will show you the prototyping template where I keep all my purpose, meaning, reason and research; where I keep it in the realm of words.

References

Williams, Tennessee. (1947). *A Streetcar Named Desire*. New York, NY: New Directions Books. Act 1, Scene 1, p. 17; Act 1, Scene 4, pp. 79–80; and Act 1, Scene 10, p. 145.

Williams, Tennessee. (2005). *A Streetcar Named Desire*. Directed by Preston Lane. Greensboro, NC: Triad Stage, The Pearl Theatre.

Word-Based Prototype Template 8

Remember, script analysis is not about analyzing our creative opinion, it precedes that. It is about analyzing the words in the script and trying to uncover the structural elements and the playwright's intention—the cogs and levers in the machine. It is about building a solid foundation on which our design can then be developed. After all, the other designers and the director are starting from the same place—the script—which helps with future collaboration but only if it truly is the same place that we are all starting from. So, we need to do our due diligence on the script analysis aspect of our design.

> P? Name - something recognizable that everyone would know, not necessarily what the sound is (e.g. lady Anne's entrance)
>> Reason (why did the playwright waste their time putting a sound cue here in the first place?)
>>> P? CHARACTER "Blah blah blah…"
>>> P? Stage direction [*blah blah blah*].
>>> ………
>> Research (what do I need to know to further understand this cue?)
>>> Blah blah even more blah.
>>> Blah blah even more blah.
>>> ……..

DOI: 10.4324/9781003223160-8

Purpose (what is so important about your sound cue that it won't get cut?)

Blah blah even more blah.
Blah blah even more blah.

....

Meaning/Feeling (how should your sound cue make the audience feel or what should they understand?)

Blah blah blah extra more blah.
Blah blah blah extra more blah.

....

Above is the template I use for all my sound cues. Notice first that there is no place to put any actual sounds. If you have kept up with my process so far, you will realize that we are not there yet. The choice of sounds comes after first understanding the intention of the cue in fine detail. Remember, we can't choose the actual sound, the *signifier*, until we have decided what needs to be *signified* and what other connotations it needs to communicate. Because it is a word-based design prototype template it can be adapted and used for all areas of design. Sound has cues but sets and props have objects and lighting has looks which can also be developed using this template. The template is easily adjusted to fit these different design specializations.

Notice secondly that I have page numbers for the cue and page numbers for every piece of support from the script. If a specific piece of dialogue or stage direction can also be used as support for another cue, I want to just be able to copy and paste it and I don't want to lose track of where it came from in the script. Also notice under the *Reason* subheading section, if a character has spoken the lines, I put their name in uppercase and quote their dialogue verbatim in quotes. Sometimes the detailed justification for a sound cue in the script emerges from a conversation rather than just a short section of dialogue, so I put down the whole conversation with page numbers, character names and quotes like it was laid out in the script. These days, copying and pasting from a pdf of the script really speeds things up. Also, under the *Reason* subheading, I list any supporting stage directions in italics and sometimes also in square parentheses if the script has written them that way.

We can change a lot about a play which is why we continue to mount different productions of the same play all the time. The one thing we are not allowed to change are the words spoken by the characters. However, stage directions can be changed and do get changed all the time. Being able to quickly differentiate between the unchangeable spoken dialogue and the changeable stage direction is very important. That is why they are listed with such an obviously different typography in my template[1].

Let's see how this works for STANLEY's entrance cue that we have been discussing above starting with the reason for the cue and the research to support it.

> **P71. STANLEY unexpectedly arrives home under the sound of the train passing**
>
> > **Reason (why did the playwright waste their time putting a sound cue here in the first place?)**
> >
> > > P7. [*The exterior of a two-story corner building on a street in New Orleans which is named Elysian Fields and runs between the L & N tracks and the river. The section is **poor** but, unlike corresponding sections in other American cities, it has a **raffish charm**. The houses are mostly white frame...*]
> > > P17. BLANCHE: "... What are you doing in a place like this?"
> > > P17. STELLA: "Now, Blanche—"
> > > P17. BLANCHE: "Oh, I'm not going to be hypocritical, I'm going to be honestly critical about it! Never, never, never in my worst dreams could I picture— Only Poe! Only Mr. Edgar Allan Poe!—could do it justice! Out there I suppose is the ghoul-haunted woodland of Weir!" [She laughs.]
> > > P17. STELLA: "No, honey, those are the L & N tracks."
> > > P30. STANLEY: "You know you can catch cold sitting around in damp things, especially when you been exercising hard like bowling is. You're a teacher, aren't you?"
> > > P30. BLANCHE: "Yes."
> > > P30. STANLEY: "What do you teach, Blanche?"
> > > P30. BLANCHE: "English."
> > > P79. [*There is a pause.*]
> > > P79. BLANCHE: "May I—speak—plainly?"

P79. STELLA: "Yes, do. Go ahead. As plainly as you want to."

P80. [*Outside, a train approaches. They are silent till the noise subsides. They are both in the bedroom. Under cover of the train's noise Stanley enters from outside. He stands unseen by the women, holding some packages in his arms, and overhears their following conversation. He wears an undershirt and grease-stained seersucker pants.*]

P80. BLANCHE: "Well—if you'll forgive me—he's common!"

P80. STELLA: "Why, yes, I suppose he is."

P80. BLANCHE: "Suppose! You can't have forgotten that much of our bringing up, Stella, that you just suppose that any part of a gentleman's in his nature! Not one particle, no! Oh, if he was just—ordinary! Just plain—but good and wholesome, but—no. There's something downright—bestial—about him! You're hating me saying this, aren't you?"

P80. STELLA: [coldly]: "Go on and say it all, Blanche."

P80. BLANCHE: "He acts like an animal, has an animal's habits...."

Research (What do I need to know to further understand?)

Play set in 1947.

the Louisville & Nashville Railroad Company

The railroad's entrance into the Gulf of Mexico ports came in 1881. A 140-mile rail line, **including roughly nine miles of trestles and bridges, linked Mobile with New Orleans**, but there was little contact with the outside world until the L&N extended its tracks to Mobile and then acquired the line on into New Orleans. This acquisition enabled the **railroad to extend its sphere of influence to international markets for agricultural products and goods manufactured in major cities along the L&N**

The postwar years brought swift, striking changes to railroading, as the **L&N, which purchased its first diesel in 1939, retired its last steam locomotive in 1957**. The L&N introduced **streamlined passenger service** with the advent of The Humming Bird and The Georgian...

Other innovations included pushbutton electronic classification **freight yards at major cities**,

"Ulalume" is a poem written by Edgar Allan Poe in 1847. Much like a few of Poe's other poems, "Ulalume" focuses on the narrator's loss of his beloved due to her death. Poe originally wrote the poem as an **elocution piece** and, as such, the poem is known for its **focus on sound**

The poem takes place on a night in the "lonesome October" with a gray sky as the leaves are withering for the autumn season. In the region of Weir, by the lake of Auber

(https://en.wikipedia.org/wiki/Ulalume)

....

That I journeyed—I journeyed down here!—
That **I brought a dread burden down here**—
On this night of all nights in the year,
Ah, what demon hath tempted me here?
Well I know, now, this dim lake of Auber—
This misty mid region of Weir—
Well I know, now, this dank tarn of Auber,
This ghoul-haunted woodland of Weir."

....

Purpose (what is so important about your sound cue that it won't get cut?)

Blah blah even more blah.
Blah blah even more blah.

....

Meaning/Feeling (how should your sound cue make the audience feel or what should they understand?)

Blah blah blah extra more blah.
Blah blah blah extra more blah.

....

Notice first that even though the cue is on page 80[2], I have also brought in stage directions and dialogue from pages 7, 17, 30 and 79. Williams, the masterful mechanism builder, has expertly distributed the exposition of this narrative element throughout the play leading up to its use. This also highlights the need for not just reading the scripts linearly as it often doesn't reveal connections across the entire piece.

Before I fill in the Purpose and the Meaning/Feeling, I want to draw attention to what the reason and the research has already made me reconsider; the words highlighted in bold. When I first read the script and started doing my analysis, I thought that the train passing would be a freight train, long and slow with the screeching sound of metal wheels against metal track and the relentless clanking sound of the couplings between the heavy freight cars. The newly married Kowalski's live in the poor end of town and the freight train would be an audible symbol of their poor surroundings; aural scenery steeped with connotation. There is certainly ample support for this in the research, but Williams also tells us that this section of town has a raffish charm. Remember this was just a few years after the end of the second world war, a time of optimism. Lives could move forward again and women like Rosie the Riveter and her serving sisters were liberated from the confinement of the home and were joining the men in their work and leisure activities. The couple is happy to be living there. They have a nice life together, bowling, and supper at Galatoire's, and then a show, with the perpetual "blue piano" wafting music from around the corner.

So instead of just a *wrong side of the tracks* trope, it could also possibly be more like a *Girl on a Train* type of environment with Elysian Fields as a desirable next level up community for newlyweds. The train is now a kind of status symbol, an indicator of their closeness to a new extended mobility and *reach* that they feel about themselves. At the start of scene 4 on page 72, after BLANCHE has been trying to paint STELLA into having "given in" on her life, STELLA says, "I'm not in anything I want to get out of". Certainly, STELLA does not act as being annoyed by the sound of the train as BLANCHE is. She accepts it as part and parcel of this new optimistic life. If that is indeed the case, there is also support in the research for a streamlined passenger service which would have the benefit of the sound coming in and going out much more quickly as the purpose of the cue requires. After all, we don't want the audience and actors to be waiting around for the cue to end before continuing the story.

This new interpretation would necessarily sound more *diddly-dah, diddly-dee* and quick passing horn than the slow lumbering screeching sounds of moving heavy freight. It would also help lay the groundwork for the soon needed second train passing in the opposite direction also symbolizing two-way mobility and vibrancy. That second train passing would allow STANLEY, who has now overheard the conversation, to leave masked by the sound and immediately return loudly as if for the first time. As we can now see, our design process exploring words as prototype has just served us well and uncovered another option that we were not originally aware of!

Focusing the production on this raffish charm as opposed to the poor setting is a directorial choice that would have implications for the whole design team. When first reading the script, we tend to believe BLANCHE's view of Elysian Fields. However, if we read what the characters who live there do and say, although it may not be the life we would choose to live, it does seem to be a vibrant optimistic life for them. It is only BLANCHE's forceful viewpoint that clouds this.

A while ago I designed the sound for two productions of *Streetcar* for two different directors in two separate theatres within a year of each other. They could not have been more different. The first production believed BLANCHE's characterization of her surroundings. The second turned out very differently and led to one of the bravest directorial moments in my career. We were halfway through tech-ing the show, well into our second act, when the director Preston Lane called for a halt. With the designers around him, he said that he was concerned that our design was just recreating our first act all over again and that it hadn't gone anywhere. He realized that rather than trying to work this out while continuing tech, we all needed to take a step back and as a design team, figure out together how we re-approach the design of our second act. He then did this amazing thing. He sent everyone else away for the afternoon, actors, technicians and management. The cost implication alone of that decision must have taken courage, but the implications were magnified even more by the loss of precious tech time to get to the first preview. That afternoon, the designers sat immersed in a silent theatre under work-lights as we retreated into our shared pre-prototype using words and discussed the whole show and different interpretations and ideas about it. We brainstormed.

This brings up an interesting point about the design process. Since it is often a refinement of ideas in tech rather than a reimagining part way through, the process that is being outlined is so important. Because we use words to prototype and then we work to define the essence of a sound concept also using words we are not locked into a specific sound, or object, or look. So, more than just a design process, as I explained in a previous chapter, it becomes a new way of thinking about design in general. Design is not about jumping quickly to choices without understanding why those choices are made, although all of us have had to do that at one time or another because there often just isn't enough time in the process to do it correctly. But look again at Lin's words at the beginning of this book, she makes exactly this point. She holds herself back from jumping to an automatic response of starting to design so she can practice a better way of design thinking.

We eventually concluded that up until the paperboy scene, it was all pretty straightforward. BLANCHE does not like this world she has found herself in including some of the characters in it. Yes, her thoughts get invaded by memories and non-reality a few times (the Varsouvianna), but it is a real world and that is the tension of the plot. However, after the paperboy scene, everything seems to get a bit more *unhinged*. The sounds and music in the stage directions seem more surreal than in our first act. Spurious odd phantomlike characters that we have never seen before now seem to bizarrely enter and exit and do surreal things. It is as if reality has been replaced by BLANCHE's view of reality. We realized that this *Muertos Flores* surrealness (as we characterized it) gave us a storytelling opportunity in the last two scenes. Like everything else, maybe the rape was not actually real. Maybe it was just BLANCHE's view of reality that we were seeing played out in front of us. This would then make the final scene with the doctor, which has always had this kind of odd tacked-on feel about it (a bit like the ending of a John Grisham novel[3]) be much more effective as it is a return to the reality that we started out with in the play.

Notice how all this was explored by the director and the design team using words, our universal collaborative prototyping medium. Using words, we could be agile prototyping our ideas and then using thought experiments we could see where they could lead us. Because of the way I document my design process as described above, I was quickly able to find support in the dialogue, stage directions, research, purpose and meaning, without having to hunt through the script every time we came up with a *what if* scenario. We eventually decided the fracture came with the scene change that preceded the entrance of the paperboy, the thunderstorm. This is the first time that BLANCHE had been alone aside from at the beginning of the play when she first entered the empty apartment before meeting STANLEY. Without STANLEY to spar with and without STELLA to rescue, she is bored and that is where we decided her fantasizing starts.

We fully embraced this scene change into the paperboy letting the thunderstorm and rain slowly build and pass in a *hot afternoon in the south* kind of way with BLANCHE on the chaise lazily leafing through magazines. The reverberant dripping from the eaves and trees that followed signified a slightly changed world. Hopping between my vocabulary and narrative view, I would eventually carry this reverb motif into every surreal *Muertos Flores* moment to symbolize the fragility of this *Paper Lantern* reality

BLANCHE was now living. Once we called everyone back, and explained what we had come up with, we went back and re-teched from the scene change into the paperboy onwards. We would eventually pull back on this concept a little and make it more ambiguous and less overt. It added to a sense of not quite being grounded which made that traditionally odd scene at the end much more integrated and powerful.

So, without listing the justifications again, here is the Purpose and Meaning/Feeling of the L&N train masking SANLEY's entrance cue.

> Purpose (what is so important about your sound cue that it won't get cut?)
>> It has to allow the audience to believe that it is masking the sound of STANLEY's entrance.
>>> Overpowering continuous sound with no gaps
>> It has to arrive quickly without seeming odd
>>> Cannot stamp on BLANCHE's line "May I–speak–plainly?".
>>> Must be in completely by the end of STELLA's "Go ahead" line.
>> It has to depart quickly without seeming odd
>> It has to not seem an unusual or distasteful sound to STELLA
>>> Should be from an already established sonic environment outside.
>>> ....

> Meaning/Feeling (how should your sound cue make the audience feel or what should they understand?)
>> ```
>> "Knowledge - Zzzzzp! Money - Zzzzzzp I - Power!
>> That's the cycle democracy is built on."
>> ``` (Jim the Gentleman Caller - *The Glass Menagerie*)
>> Raffish Charm. Gentrified starter community by the tracks
>>> Fast. Express. Streamlined Passenger service
>>> Leisure & mobility not just commerce
>>> Liberation from the past. A different world from the world
>> STELLA and BLANCHE were brought up in
>>> Vibrant and optimistic. Victory. Peacetime.
>>> Bestial - as in gleaming, precise and powerful (not dark)

When I share this method with students, they often mix up Purpose with Meaning and vice versa. This comes from a high school background of teachers trying to develop the student's creativity by discussing and justifying sound cues from the standpoint of what emotional contribution they are providing to the production. Because of this, I have developed a clear litmus test to separate Purpose from Meaning. If we move our sound cue to another part of the script away from the position it was intended for, then it is its purpose that changes not its meaning. So, if I moved the sound of the L&N train passing and place it somewhere else, it clearly would not fulfill the purpose of covering the sound of STANLEY's entrance though it would still convey the same Meaning/Feeling. In contrast, if I change the content of a cue and keep its original position, then it is its meaning that changes. So, if I instead replace the sound of the L&N train passing with the sound of a New Orleans Jazz Band passing outside, as we have already discussed earlier its Meaning/Feeling changes although the purpose—its intended function—of covering STANLEY's entrance would stay the same.

The L&N train passing either has the meaning of the-wrong-side-of-the-tracks or an up-and-coming neighborhood as we have discussed above, but a New Orleans Jazz Band conveys Mardi Grass party time or funeral which clearly is at odds with the meaning the dialogue is delivering at that place in the script. So, in short, the Purpose gets broken if the cue gets moved and the designed Meaning changes if the sound is replaced by a different sound. It is usually Purpose that we find more difficult to grasp because we probably have never had our eyes opened to see a sound cue in this way, as another small cog in a giant intricate interconnected mechanism. Every cog is there for a purpose.

Playwrights bake-in structure as well as meaning into their scripts so either of these can be motivation for a cue. As I have already said, the reason a cue gets cut is nothing to do with the playwright's intention, it is to do with running out of tech time. After all, we are designers. Given enough time and money, we can make almost anything work! Therefore, if the motivation for a new cue is purely Meaning/Feeling, we also need to identify a purpose; a cog that fits into the mechanism that is already there. If we consider the penultimate scene change in *A Streetcar Named Desire* described earlier, we can clearly see that it was originally meaning that motivated the telephone cue in the first place. The purpose, the cog, was fabricated out of parts that were already present to fit a missing opportunity—a space for that cog in the machine provided by the playwright; that the hospital would call when the baby was delivered. It is the indecision and eventual ignoring of that telephone ringing that triggered the meaning with its resulting emotional rollercoaster. Also realize that the insistent ringing would continue unanswered as the lights went down on the scene with the cries from BLANCHE, and STANLEY's hateful dialogue being eventually overwhelmed by the scene change music.

Notes

1 We could also use colors to differentiate between dialogue and stage directions instead of using typographical emphasis but since it is only two things that we are differentiating between we may want to save the use of different colors for a situation where we want to quickly differentiate between more than two different things.
2 Taken from Williams, T. (1947) *A Streetcar Named Desire*, New Directions Books.
3 I really enjoy his books but I always feel like the publisher has stepped in and told Grisham to end it quickly so they can publish it.

References

Poe, Edgar A. (December 1847). Ulalume. In The American Review, edited by Edgar A. Poe. No. 36, George H. Colton, New York. Lines 87 to 94.

Williams, Tennessee. (1945). *The Glass Menagerie*. New York, NY: New Directions Books. Scene 7.

Williams, Tennessee. (1947). *A Streetcar Named Desire*. New York, NY: New Directions Books. Act 1, Scene 1, p. 7 & p. 17; Act 1, Scene 4, p. 72 & pp. 79–80; and Act 1, Scene 10, p. 145.

Williams, Tennessee. (2005). *A Streetcar Named Desire*. Directed by Preston Lane, Greensboro, NC: Triad Stage, The Pearl Theatre.

Simplicity, Syncing Up and Annealing   9

As we can see from the previous chapter unveiling my epiphany about the L&N train sound cue, this word-based prototype is a living document. All that I have detailed about this one specific sound cue is still not the final product. It is constantly being developed further as I learn more relevant things from my research, as I have more discussions with the director and as I see the preliminary work from my fellow designers. I am writing it only for me to see and not for others. I don't worry about spelling or grammar at this point. I want to know that I understand the justification, research, purpose and meaning of any sound cue when talking with the director and other designers. I may not understand the cue fully yet, but I don't ever want to be in a position of playing catch-up in these discussions. That is not to say that I don't want to learn something new from these discussions, but they have contacted me because I am the expert, so I need to do my due diligence and work expertly. But, as I said, that doesn't mean it is not constantly changing. Remember, it is a design process, not a design product. *Prototype as a process not a prototype as a product.* It is never a finished document. This word-based prototype eventually gets overtaken by actual sounds that I start assembling and editing on my laptop and is finally complete by opening night.

These documents can get quite complex as ideas and justifications get piled one on top of another for every sound cue in the whole play. But an interesting thing occurs in the process of hopping between Narrative (the cues in sequence) and Vocabulary (the groups of similar cues) and further refining the ideas so that they work perfectly in both domains. The complexity, which has been increasing steadily throughout the process,

DOI: 10.4324/9781003223160-9

suddenly collapses in upon itself—as if under its own weight. And we are left with a kind of simplicity, a unification of all the myriad details reformed into a simpler underlying structure. This occurrence is not a new thing, it happens all the time. It also happens in other fields where complexity seems to proliferate while trying to fully understand something. Look at what the late theoretical physicist Dr. Richard Feynman said.

> every once in a while we have these integrations when everything's pulled together into a unification, in which it turns out to be simpler than it looked before.

Seeing the long seemingly unending formulas across multiple chalkboards, working out the math(s) for quantum physics and quantum electrodynamics, we can see that it can get very complex indeed. It gets similarly as complex[1] as what we are trying to do working at our granular level on the script.

Before I went into theatre, I used to be an assistant research chemist. As an assistant, I mostly got to do the *grunt* work that takes time and is usually not very exciting. One of those tasks was getting pure crystals from saturated solutions. I would have a glass flask full of a mixture of compounds dissolved in a saturated solution (the product of some reaction) and I would scratch away at the submerged inside surface of the flask with a glass rod. Sometimes I had to do this off and on for weeks trying to seed the formation of a pure crystal that would then grow. It was a technique for separating out chemicals in their pure form. Nothing would happen for ages as I scratched away but then suddenly, a minute crystal would form. Once crystallization had started, I didn't have to scratch anymore as a crystal only attracts out of the solution the same compound that the crystal is made of. The crystal would grow bigger until all that specific compound was now solid and in its pure form leaving the other compounds—the impurities—still dissolved in the solution.

It seems the same thing happens when hopping between Narrative and Vocabulary and *scratching* away at our design. Nothing seems to happen for a long time then suddenly, a minute piece of design sense emerges and everything else starts to coalesce around it and fall into place. It is beautiful watching crystals grow in a flask, just as beautiful as witnessing the collapsing to simplicity when a design starts to take shape.

Notice that unlike with crystallization, the original quest is not to find the underlying simplicity per se; it is a quest to fully understand everything in minute detail and find the links between often very different ideas. The collapsing to simplicity is an *Aha!* moment, a *now I realize what is going on* moment. There is work done leading up to it and work needing to be done after it. If we are forcing the work to try to get to what should after all be a natural collapse into simplicity, we may inadvertently invent a collapse where there is none. We may end up scratching the wrong compound out of the solution and may end up forcing something into an underlying structure that is not there.

Allowing this collapsing to simplicity to happen naturally in its own time becomes a milestone of sorts for my design process. It is at this point that I know I have a credible design. Up until this point, I am trying to understand everything—I am working toward a design, but I know it isn't a design yet. After this collapse, I now have a design that I am trying to flesh out to its fullest by finding other opportunities in the play to use the design elements that have crystallized out of solution. If the collapse happens too early in the process, I end up with not enough understanding to sustain a whole design. If it happens too late in the process, there is no time to develop the design to its fullest potential.

The kind of work leading up to the collapse is different from the kind of work after the collapse. If for some reason the *Aha!* moment is not obvious, it is this change in the type of the work I am doing that is recognizable indicating that a collapse has occurred. I never force it and I never get worried that it hasn't happened yet. The more expert and practiced I have become at my specific process of design, the more consistently it happens. Remember, design is a process. Although it is hard work, we should embrace it, and not try and force it.

Other designers as well as the director are also engaging in their own process(es) during this period so the act of periodically coming together or communicating with each other and getting back into sync as described earlier becomes the *ticking clock* for this process. If we have luxuriated too long on one section of our process, when we get back into sync, we realize we need to catch up. Conversely, we may realize we are in advance of where the others are when we all sync up[2] so we can afford to luxuriate a little longer on the next step of our process. It is these mile markers and not any rigid schedule that help us stay on time during the process.

Heading up the sound program at UNCSA made it inconvenient for me to take design jobs far from school, so I have spent the last decade working mainly for the same director at the same theatre in the next town over. As such, the timing of the process for me is always the same and it has become part of my baked in DNA as a designer. On the odd occasion when I did design further afield and on a different production schedule than I was used to, it is these mile markers that kept me on track. So, trust in them and have faith in the process.

This trust in the process is such a tough concept for students. At first, students trust it because they trust their teachers, this is like a second-hand trust. However, before long they need to go through a period of doubt to emerge with a better understanding of the process that they can then trust to do what it is designed to do. They now have enough experience to have firsthand trust in themselves.

When I was a child, I loved to draw fantastical spaceships and underwater vehicles. This was probably a product of watching *Stingray* and *Thunderbirds* (British TV's endearingly quirky attempt at Sci-Fi). In the top left-hand corner of a clean new page in my exercise book, I would start drawing a new spaceship or submarine. Predictably, I would soon realize that I had made a mistake or would realize that if it had such-and-such it would be even better. I would turn over the page and start a new drawing on a fresh clean page. We all undoubtedly recognize this behavior in our younger selves and in children around us. This process of always starting again from scratch when we make a mistake or change our mind is a valid learning process. Indeed, as we are learning to flex our creative muscle, it serves us well as it forces us to practice getting to the same point over and over again. But this practice of repeatedly covering the same ground doesn't seem to be a very good process for helping us move much further beyond this nascent ability. The next idea or mistake and we are back to the beginning again.

It is easy to start over again from scratch as we sketch out our spaceship. However, imagine the time and cost involved if we are a city planner and every time that we made a mistake or had a better idea, we discarded the work we had already accomplished and started the whole process again from scratch? The issue is immediately obvious without having to spell it out. So, we as designers develop other different processes for solving creative problems that would serve us better. A different valid creative problem-solving process would be to keep what works and only improve the parts that need it. This is a design process of optimization and continual improvement rather than always starting again from scratch.

But, as we can imagine, there are many possible ways of accomplishing continual improvement. For instance, instead of just improving the parts that need it, we could discard them entirely and start those parts again from scratch. This is essentially what the director Preston Lane did when tech-ing the second act of *A Streetcar Named Desire* as outlined in an earlier chapter. Or we could slightly change different parts of that piece creating many different options and assessing which option is stronger and then move in that direction with other small changes. Processes are just formalized ways of doing something that can be chosen and applied to the task at hand. There are, in fact, many different formalized ways of optimizing a design and some are more helpful than others in any given situation.

As a culture, we are losing this ability to improve something; to fix it instead of just throwing it out. We are bombarded every day by advertising and advice that compels us to devalue or discard what is not working perfectly and to desire or buy the new latest one. For a consumer, this is an act of always starting from scratch and we can see the cost in the form of unimaginable waste and the unsustainable destruction of resources. It is a wonder that any designer can practice a process of optimization while living a process of continually starting from scratch. Unfortunately, the truth is that designers who can do this are becoming few and far between. Watch any home decorating show and the "designers" usually completely throw out what they are confronted with and put in something brand new. On one level it makes sense. Advertisers don't want their products to be permanent, they want us to buy their latest version and throw away what we have previously purchased as their investors require more revenue. But the ability of optimization is being bred out of us. Drip, drip, drip.

The formalized process that best describes my way of designing as laid out above is called *Simulated Annealing*. A clear description of this process of optimization is by the philosopher Daniel Dennett in his 1995 book Darwin's Dangerous Idea; Evolution and the Meanings of Life. (see quotation below).

> ...consider the process of annealing a piece of metal to temper it.... The blacksmith repeatedly heats the metal and then lets it cool, and somehow in the process it becomes much stronger... As the metal cools from its molten state, the solidification starts in many different spots at the same time, creating crystals that grow together until the whole is solid. But the first time this happens, the arrangement of the individual crystal structures is suboptimal—weakly held together, and with lots of internal stresses and strains. Heating it up again—but not all the way to melting—partially breaks down these structures, so that, when they are permitted to cool the next time, the broken-up bits will adhere to the still-solid bits in a different arrangement. It can be

proven mathematically that these rearrangements will tend to get better and better, approaching the optimum or strongest total structure, provided the regime of heating and cooling has the right parameters. So powerful is this optimization procedure that it has been used as the inspiration for an entirely general problem-solving technique…—"simulated annealing," which has nothing to do with metals or heat, but is just a way… to build, disassemble, and rebuild a… structure…over and over, blindly groping towards a better—indeed, an optimal—version.

Hopefully, what I have described of my own design process so far—keeping sound in words, exposing the underlying cogs (Narrative. Vocabulary. Purpose. Meaning. Justification. Research.), and continually adjusting the words so that they fit two (or more) different views perfectly—is akin to heating the design up but not melting it all. The bits that do melt are weak bits. Letting it cool again anneals those bits and gets it stronger each time. I don't throw it all out and start from scratch each time, I don't go at it willy-nilly or pray for the muse to be close to me that day, I practice a very specific formalized process of creative development and problem solving, a very resilient form of design optimization. It is a design process that serves me well.

I even use this simulated annealing process in my writings such as with this book. I first write down all that I want to say—verbose, messy, poor grammar, duplications and gaps. I then write a sentence in bold at the start of each paragraph that sums up the one idea of the paragraph. If there seems to be more than one idea in the paragraph, I split it into as many smaller paragraphs as there are different ideas within it, and then give each single focus paragraph its own descriptive sentence in bold. I then sequentially list all these descriptive sentences in bold and move them around to achieve a better flow of cogent argument (my version of heating them up). I then discard what now seems superfluous to the thrust of the argument and I also fill in the gaps that have now been exposed. I then substitute the sentences with the actual paragraph and go through every word making it clearer and more succinct. I then send it to two of my very good friends who suggest ways of making it clearer. The publishers then submit it, and the technical reviewers go through it and ask me to make changes to improve it. All these stages are simulated annealing, heating and cooling—strengthening. Eventually, it is published, and you read it.

Notes

1 I am talking about complexity not importance.
2 There may be a tendency to advance the others to where we are during sync up but remember, the journey is important for all designers, so it is best not to circumvent that journey for them just because we find ourselves in advance of where they are. Instead, we should use the sync up to really listen to them and check that we haven't missed anything.

References

Dennett, D. (1995). *Darwin's Dangerous Idea; Evolution and the Meanings of Life*. London, UK: Penguin Books. p. 57.

Feynman, R. (1999). *The Pleasure of Finding Things Out: The Best Short Works of Richard P. Feynman*. Cambridge, MA: Perseus Books. p. 14.

On-Ramp, Quest and Warm-Up

10

There is this cultural stereotype that creativity is a gift and that it just seems to happen for those *chosen* few and therefore doesn't require any rigor. Watching the documentaries in our Innovation and Creativity class, we all witness the incredible amount of work and effort that these creative people put into developing their own creative process to continue to be successful. Lawrence Muganga in his 2018 book *You Can't Make Fish Climb Trees* describes how Sir Ken Robinson and others are continually advocating that creativity is not an innate talent you either have or not, but instead is a process people can learn and can improve upon. I know as an educator that I sometimes have trouble convincing new students to see the value in a rigorous design process and fully engage in it. That is, to actually *do the work*. This is understandable as the students' usually come in thinking that they were accepted into our conservatory training program because of the talents that they already possess or the talents we (apparently mistakenly)[1] thought they possessed. The fact is that we accepted them, not because of any supposed talent but because we honestly assessed that they would respond well to our method of conservatory training and as a result, they would add value to themselves as creative practitioners in the industry.

I see this *innate talent* vs *process* playout in most of the productions I attend that have been designed by a student or early career professional. No matter what the field of design, I always seem to be left feeling that the initial "cool" design idea would have served the show much better if it had been allowed to go on a collaborative creative journey and end up

DOI: 10.4324/9781003223160-10

66 On-Ramp, Quest and Warm-Up

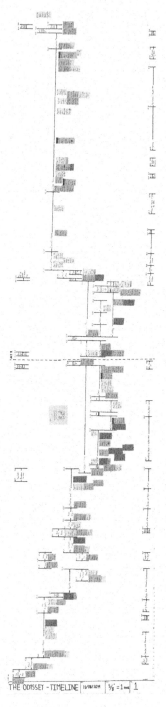

Fig 10.1. *The Odyssey* timeline visualization by William Barney. (A horizontal image of a skeletal timeline with post-it notes attached to it.)

somewhere even better. Too often, initial design ideas are produced on stage in these productions because of time and scheduling restrictions. *Cool* is instantaneous whereas *serving a show* takes time. Because of this, I have developed an on-ramp for these students to show them the value of putting effort into developing a design from the script instead of just using their immediate creative opinion.

I get the sound design students to draw out a timeline of the script marking off the pages and then add to it scenes and notable events as well as sound and music cues. Depending on the type of script, the timeline produces layers above and below it that refer to either different realities, or different places or situations etc. This gives us a *big picture* view of the whole drama that is hard to get from just reading the script or listening to the recording or watching the play. It turns something that is time based into an immediately perceivable presentational analogue of the whole play where one can *see* the beginning middle and end all at once without waiting to get to that part. I usually get the students to start mapping it out on a white board until they figure out how they want to lay it out and then give them a long roll of paper to do it on.

Figure 10.1 is an example of one of these timelines by one of my sound design students, William Barney. It is for the play *The Odyssey* by Mary Zimmerman, a modern rendering of the classic. The actual scroll is probably 15 feet in length (4 to 5 meters). At this scale, it is impossible to read so I have also included a small closeup section from Figure 10.2 below. As we can see, Barney chose to use the layers for indicating the level of storytelling. Characters start telling a story that they then start acting out and within that story that they are now acting out they start telling another story that they then start acting out: story within story within story. It is this artifice that allows Zimmerman to compress the whole Odyssey into a manageable and enjoyable two-hour play. Barney also uses post-it notes on this skeleton to insert his ideas for cues.

By laying it out in this way, aspects of the intricate underlying mechanism that would not normally be obvious become exposed. We can see that the journey returns to where it started from with the Muse on Mount Olympus. Odysseus returns home but now changed from his journey (his odyssey). We can see that the narrative is laid out in three distinct acts even though it will be performed with only one intermission as is the current custom. We can also see that a lot seems to happen in the first two acts and not as much in the third act until near the end. This is a problem with many plays that modern productions must somehow overcome. Just sit through any Eugene O'Neill play to see what I mean!

68 On-Ramp, Quest and Warm-Up

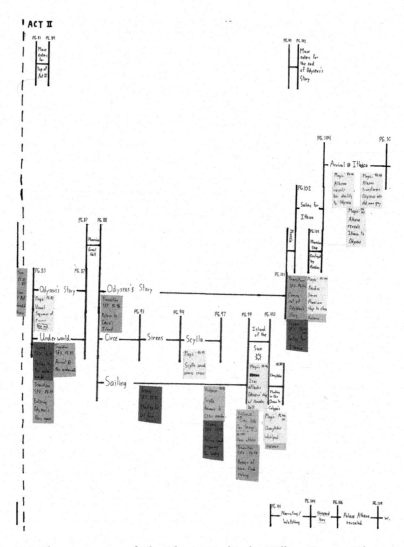

Fig 10.2. Close up section of *The Odyssey* timeline by William Barney. (Close up view of the timeline showing design ideas written on the attached post it notes.)

We can see that this is in fact another form of prototype. The timeline is fixed as it is sequential with the pages, as are the levels of storytelling within the play. These become the skeleton on which to hang the ideas. It is the post-it notes that are changeable and allow for evolution of the ideas for the cues. The scroll also allows for collaboration and the timeline becomes a kind of immediately perceivable *Rosetta Stone*, a common ground for all the different designers to use to discuss their own design ideas as they share them with the others. This is in fact what happened in this production[2]. The director and other designers used this timeline that was generated by this process of the sound designer to inform and communicate all their ideas and decisions. Since it is the starting point for the *Narrative-Vocabulary-Purpose-Meaning* prototype process using words, it is one of the first things that becomes available for the whole design team to use. The early bird gets the worm! I would argue that this is a much better and exciting *way in* or starting point for a design than the traditional method of finding a stimulus as a *way in* and hoping that the next steps will somehow become apparent. *Stimulus is not process!* Anything can be a stimulus. Successful reproducible processes are what the investors behind producers pay for. Design as opposed to art is all about mitigating financial risk!

So, we may ask, how do we get from this living document of design-prototype-using-words to delivering sounds in tech? Once the collapse to simplicity has happened and the words have been through further stages of refinement necessitated by this collapse, we are in a much better position to go looking for and assembling sound effects. I consider all that I have done up to this point the act of *suiting-up*. I think of the process of collaborative design we practice in a fanciful *Knights* and *Quest* kind of way[3]. A director has been tasked with the *Quest* of doing battle with the *Dragon* (the play). She has assembled a worthy group of *Knights* to assist her. Their job is to suit up in the best armor possible and know their enemy having done as much research as possible. Then they do battle alongside of the director. However, there is still one thing missing.

One of the final acts of suiting up before I show up is to prepare to be creative. To warm up. An aspect of the cultural stereotype that creativity is a gift mentioned earlier is that people don't think it requires any warm-up process. Since designing really is a rigorous practice like any other, I have found that warming up makes a noticeable difference. I learned this in an earlier incarnation of the Innovation and Creativity class. I made an offer to any of the students attending the class that if they met me at Borders Books (now sadly gone) an hour before the start of class I would buy them the beverage of their choice. Borders Books, as well as having a good coffee shop also had an extensive magazine rack. There were magazines covering subjects I never even knew existed. Each week I tasked the students to pick up a magazine on something that they would never normally be interested in and had no previous knowledge about and spend the first half hour reading it while drinking their beverage of choice.

The last half of this *pre*-class was for them to pick an article out of their magazine and without the aid of the magazine share with the rest of the group what they learned or found interesting in the article and then we would briefly discuss it. Notice how they weren't allowed to read it, they had to retell it in their own words and discuss what they learned about it. I noticed that later in class, the discussion and insights from the students that had warmed up was on a higher level than the students who hadn't warmed up. Of course, it may have just been because of the coffee! However, if I was a collaborator, it would have been more fun and interesting working with the students who had warmed up.

There is sometimes confusion between warm-up and practice when applied to creativity. The two sometimes get mistaken for each other. The difference between the two is more easily understood if we consider something like running a marathon. To practice running a marathon, we need to run increasingly longer distances until we can run just over 22 miles. Even when we can already achieve this distance, we sometimes choose to run shorter distances for practice, to keep our body fit and prepared without needlessly potentially damaging our joints etc. However, the day we compete in a marathon we probably do not run a marathon before the race starts. We do probably run a shorter distance, stretch, carbo load (eat pasta), take in extra salt, exercise aerobically and get our muscles fluid and moving. As we can see, the work involved in warm-up and in practice is actually very different and distinct. The same is true for designing. We practice designing by designing, but we don't warm up by designing. We warm up by practicing something very different and distinct.

I have a very specific process of warm-up that I practice before I start choosing sounds. I allow myself two whole days disappearing down rabbit holes on the internet. Two *whole* days. During those days, I don't do any other work on my sound design, and I spend all day warming up this way. My process is that I start with something I find interesting and click on links or use associated searches to explore it either deeper or peripherally. In the process, I find something else that piques my interest and I disappear down that rabbit hole too. I do not save any links or make notes of anything I find. I'm not even going in directions that would serve the play or my design. To be honest, only a small fraction of what I find is even audio. I don't even purposely try to remember where I found anything of interest. It is not the finding of something that is important in my warm-up process although everything that I discover I find fascinating. It is the journeying that I am practicing; actively trying never to get stuck or go in circles. If I inadvertently end up in a place I have been before, I head off in another direction.

Another aspect also emerges because of the time I commit to this warm-up process. Over the two days a sense of the whole *cultural terrain* emerges, its interconnectedness, where it is we are and what this world looks like at this specific point in time… this momentary disruption between history and future that we inhabit. Before the ease of the internet, I would visit Art galleries and Museums. I would wander the Musée d'Orsay, The Louvre and the Pompidou Center just to bathe in their collections and the ideas they provoke in me. Before that, it was photo magazines like National Geographic, Time-Life and Paris Match. The pantheon of Art and culture is an analogue of the evolving world in miniature, its past, how it imagined the future would be and where we are now; how that future eventually unfolded.

I have now finally completed my suiting up. Now I show up. I use my Vocabulary view to start assembling my ingredients. After all, I now know that I need *this* type of sound that will fulfill *this* specific purpose and convey *this* specific meaning and that I will need *these* different instances of it that make *this* kind of journey. Think about it. This is powerful stuff to have figured out before we start the usual flailing around looking for sound effects. My warm-up has made me very agile and has also unconsciously influenced me so as I go looking, a character starts to emerge in my choices. This then becomes the character of this specific design. It is different from the character of my other designs because this specific warm-up journey was unique, and this play and production and team are unique. Character emerges. It is never forced. So, at this stage, I assemble the ingredients. I first find, then edit and group together the sound effects I will need, but I don't construct them into sound cues yet. For that, I wait until I have watched the designer run. For now, I just leave them as prepared ingredients ready to use.

Notes

1 I know that some students feel like fakes even though we see in them what they sometimes cannot see themselves.
2 Although fully realized, built and loaded into the theatre, this production was never teached as UNCSA went to remote learning because of COVID-19. It was eventually loaded out and *dumpstered* without ever being performed.
3 I apologize that there is not a more gender inclusive or gender-neutral example I can use.

References

Barney, W. (2020). *The Odyssey by Mary Zimmerman.* Timeline Visualization. Unpublished class project.

Muganga, L. (2018). *You Can't Make Fish Climb Trees: Overcoming Educational Malpractice.* Victoria, Canada: Friesen Press. p. 105.

Meet & Greet 11

Before we continue with innovating the design implementation process from the designer run onward, let's go back to the *Meet & Greet* to clear something up that worries a lot of students and early career designers especially those of us designing lighting, sound and projections. Traditionally, the Meet & Greet is on the first day of rehearsals. It is an opportunity for the actors, administration, staff, designers, technicians and some of the board members and investors to meet each other. The reception is usually followed by welcome speeches and the director giving their vision for the production. The design presentations then follow. Finally, most people are ejected from the room and the actors, stage managers, dramaturges and the director get down to the first readthrough and then the start of rehearsals.

Here in the US, most theatre designer contracts follow the United Scenic Artists (USA) contract either directly or in essence. As the name suggests, the professional association was originally just for Scenic designers so the timeline in the contract was originally built around their deliverables. In regional theatre, the building of the set usually starts at the same time as rehearsals start. This means that the set design needs to be finished by the Meet & Greet and can now be fully unveiled and presented with foam core models and renderings. Costumes follow a similar timeline and can also present finished renderings and swatches during the Meet & Greet. As with sets, most of costumes' build will be after rehearsals start when actors are on site and can attend fittings etc. So, for sets and costumes, the design needs to be finished by the Meet & Greet so that the build can start.

DOI: 10.4324/9781003223160-11

But what of lighting? A large part of the lighting design will be as a response to the rehearsal process which hasn't happened yet. How can a lighting designer (LD) decide where to point a lighting fixture if the director hasn't yet reached that scene in rehearsals and blocked the actor to be there yet? Certainly, by the Meet & Greet, the theatre and playing space are known as is the set, so we can construct a lighting delivery system that could cover all eventualities. We also know the script and have contributed to the design discussions, so we can probably choose our colors (gels) and gobos and have some idea about the sequence of *looks* we would like to achieve as well as any *specials* that we will need to accomplish them.

If you have spent any time in tech, you will have witnessed how hard the LD, their assistant and the board operator work on meticulously building each cue and its transition. There is a perennial joke in the industry *"waiting for sound"*. But, if we were to add up the amount of time each takes, more tech time is spent these days waiting for lighting than sound. It is only that lighting do their work over headsets so everyone can listen to them diligently building each cue. Also, waiting for lighting to build each cue is an accepted part of the tech process from the days when scenic designers also used to design lights (and costumes). Sound, projections and automation are relatively new fields, so we have some *dues* to be paid in the form of receiving some teasing, usually harmless unless egos escalate it into shaming.

Certainly, we have all noticed during tech how it seems to be this very work done by lighting, sound and projections in responding to what the actors are doing on stage that seems to produce what we would all consider to be the design. So how can we present this design at the Meet & Greet before tech has happened? The answer is that we don't, and in practice, we are not required to. What we do need to have completed by then is at least a first stab at the paperwork for a system so it can be costed out and rigged. The problem is that explaining in detail the system that is going to be implemented and showing this paperwork is the last thing all these people at the Meet & Greet want to hear and see.

As an educator, I get to see a lot of beautifully drafted lighting plots. In the school of Design and Production (D&P) here at UNCSA, every student presents their portfolio to every member of faculty, even faculty from outside their discipline, at the end of every academic year to show the progress they have made. However, having also attended most of the shows worked on by these students, I also get to see with my own eyes the different lighting designs that these beautifully drafted lighting plots produce. I see accomplished ones, unremarkable ones, first attempts, etc. I am amazed that even though their designs, and the quality of their designs, on stage vary wildly, to my non-expert eyes, all their lighting plots look similar to me. The truth is that a person who doesn't do theatre lighting cannot really tell from the lighting plot how the design will end up, so showing those assembled at the Meet & Greet, the paperwork and talking about the system are not really going to give the attendees a vision to get behind.

My suggestion is that since the Meet & Greet is really part of the design process, treat it as another opportunity to innovate for better outcomes. Ask ourselves, "what do I want these people to hear"? Even though we designers and the director are already well into our own design journey by then, the reason for this meeting is to mark the start of a journey for those attending. The people at the Meet & Greet want to hear that everyone is on the same page and heading in the same direction. They want to get a feel for some sense of momentum and support to start them off and take them through what will be an exhausting process to get to the opening night. They want a vision of the end-product to head toward and they want to know that their contribution to that end-product will be encouraged and valued. So, let us give them that. Give them what we ourselves would want to be given at the Meet & Greet.

Use the universal pre-prototype medium of words that we have already developed and tell them about what we are going to achieve. Tell them how excited we are to be part of this amazing production. Tell them about what we have learned so far in our own design journey that will help others. A lot more important people will have spoken before us so pick out some things from what they have said to reinforce and show solidarity as a design team. Frame what we say as a way of our own design specialization reinforcing and supporting the contribution of the other design specializations in the overall show. Be a nice person! The last thing that is needed in a show that is starting out is someone who plainly does not want to fit in. Remember to be quick. The Meet & Greet is not meant to be just about you!

The Meet & Greet is meant to be about engagement in a vision. After all, the set designer usually doesn't present their build drawings at the Meet & Greet, they present their model. They present something that the attendees can quickly and immediately grasp and engage with. Something that those attending can project themselves into whether their role is selling tickets or acting on the stage. This brings up an important point. An actor will not try and *Act* at the Meet & Greet. You would not expect them to. They don't have to prove that they are an actor at that initial meeting. Everyone already accepts that they are. So, in situations like this, realize that we don't have to prove that we are an LD, or a sound designer etc. People already accept that we are, that is why we were hired. That is the reason why we are there. Realize that everyone else is just doing what you are doing at these meetings. They are trying to get a sense of the other people. Can we trust each other? Are we approachable? Are we friendly? Are we all fellow passengers on a journey? So, figure out what we ourselves are trying to find out about the others around us and display these qualities ourselves.

One last thing, if you are a sound designer, I suggest you don't attempt to play them any sound! I mean it! You may have noticed that in most corporate presentations and big events such as political debates, it is usually the sound that has problems or seems more unpolished than the visuals. To get sound that will not sound crappy, or weak, or fail in some way takes set-up time and specialized equipment and manning by technicians. None of these are usually available at a Meet & Greet as no other design area is requiring any similar level of technical support. Anyway, the sound is so reliant on context that it is meaningless outside of its eventual place in the show, so I never even bother playing any sound. Also, when sound has problems or fails, it has the ability to annoy not just disappoint. A design presentation is a high-profile moment. Best not to take any needless chances.

This is not because sound isn't considered as important as the other design areas. It is. It is just that in my experience the Meet & Greet is not the place or the crowd to share it with. A while ago, the famous sound designer Jonathan Deans shared with me how when he starts each design for Cirque du Soleil, he would put together a CD of sound and music ideas and send it to his producers and design collaborators. This is obviously a valid practice even though it still suffers from the absence of context that sound is so reliant on. However, realize that this is a much more targeted group of people than would be present at the Meet & Greet. Also, listening privately to a CD or streamed sound file is a very different experience than hearing it in a large room with a group of seemingly random people. Knowing how long Cirque[1] took to develop their shows, Jonathan's CD delivery would potentially predate the Meet & Greet by years!

If I need to present anything at the Meet & Greet, I describe it using words. As discussed previously, I allow others to *buy into* my design by completing the vision in their head or in this case the sound. Remember, we are essentially collaborating with all the people at the Meet & Greet so use what we have learned so far about our own design process. Also, if you have innovated your own design process to be aligned with mine, then you probably won't have any sound to play at the Meet & Greet since you will not have built any cues yet!

There is one situation when playing something at the Meet & Greet would be appropriate and that is if you have composed or assembled any music for the show. Humans spend their whole life engaging with music, so we are good at getting a sense of music even from the small loudspeakers on a laptop. As a teenager, I could still hear Paul McCartney's bass guitar even through a small Sony transistor radio where the loudspeaker was so small it was physically not able to reproduce those frequencies. We humans are amazing, and our perception can compensate for these things. That bass guitar is there for us even though we shouldn't be able to hear it[2]. Our mind completes the picture, or in this case, the sound. This perceptual completion will also happen when music is played from a laptop.

If you do play music at the Meet & Greet, remember to heavily compress it so everyone can hear it. Remember, there is usually a lot of background noise at a Meet & Greet as people whisper with their colleagues as they get excited about what they are finding out. Don't play them any of the subtle stuff, play the major thematic elements and/or rhythms. Play them something aspirational and inspirational. People march to the beat of the drum and the melody of the pipes. If anyone wants to hear more, we can let them hear it later over headphones or by giving them access to it online. Be courteous, remember to make a point of showing them that we are wiping down the headphones when sharing them between people (especially in the world we now live in).

Jordan Kerner, the film producer of the movie *Fried Green Tomatoes*, told me the story of how they specifically contracted Thomas Newman to compose the music before they even started shooting. Usually, the composer only starts working after everything has been shot and edited. Newman's music for the movie is very evocative, a musical arabesque of an oboe representing one of the main characters and a clarinet representing the other. Kerner recalls that he and the Director Jon Avnet played the music to the two lead actors before they shot each scene to help them build these beautifully nuanced delicate characters. On a considerably much lesser scale, I composed some film noir thematic music for a production of *Dial 'M' for Murder* and I found that everyone in the theatre was whistling the main tune throughout the whole process, even after the show closed. As I have said, if we give them marching music, people will march.

If you are offered the chance, I suggest that you always attend the readthrough after the Meet & Greet. Professional actors have usually already learned at least half their lines and have started developing their character by the first readthrough, so it is like listening to a radio drama or podcast. It is always a real pleasure. Hearing the words spoken out loud is a totally different experience than reading them yourself and much closer to what an eventual audience will experience during the show. I always find it amazing at what becomes audible that didn't jump off the page previously when just reading the script myself. Make a note of anything that is exposed that you would like to remember. Also realize that as we are hearing it for the first time, we ourselves are also resonating and engaging with the material as an audience would. This aspect is just as important to understand for our design as are the specific things that become audible from the readthrough, so also make a note of this. Since we will still be working on our *Narrative-Vocabulary-Purpose-Meaning-Annealing* prototype process, update and include anything we discover.

Notes

1 UNCSA had a long relationship with Cirque du Soleil as a *feeder* school.
2 We hear the transient at the start of a bass note coupled with the higher harmonics that can be reproduced by a small loudspeaker and then we reconstruct the fundamental bass note in our mind.

References

Avnet, J. (Director) & Kerner, J (Producer). (1991). *Fried Green Tomatoes* [Motion Picture]. Universal City, CA: Universal Pictures.
Knott, Frederick. (2011). *Dial 'M' for Murder*. Directed by Preston Lane. Greensboro, NC: Triad Stage, The Pearl Theatre.
United Scenic Artists • Local USA 829, IATSE.

Designer Run   12

The next phase is the design implementation process, and this starts with the designer run. Typically, at least in regional theatre here in the USA, the designer run happens at the end of the last day of rehearsal so the actors can go home immediately afterward and get a day off before tech starts. As information comes thick and fast during a designer run, I have innovated my process to make sure that I don't miss anything. Even if I have been using an electronic pdf of the script up to this point, I usually ask for a hard copy for the designer run. Over the years, I have developed some very specific requirements for this hard copy of the script.

- Portrait orientation.
- One page of the script per side with the reverse side blank (if it doesn't already come that way).
- Hole punch the script on the right-hand side and not the left.

I then invert all the pages one by one while keeping them all in sequence so that the script side is facing downward with page one at the top of the pile and the last page at the bottom. Now when it is loaded into a ring binder, the script now presents with each page of dialogue on the left and the blank rear side of the next page on the right. Because I am right-handed, this allows me to make quick scribbles in pencil on the blank side without taking my eyes off the run and without messing up the printed dialogue on the left. If I need to draw quick lines over to the blank side from dialogue or words where things should start and should

DOI: 10.4324/9781003223160-12

stop, I do. Also, if I need to draw one or more vertical lines on the blank side showing that a sound or underscore is continuing through dialogue, I can. Since I am the only one having to interpret what I am scribbling, I employ my personal shorthand that allows me to be fast. This isn't anything complex or fancy. I just have to remember what it refers to and take as little time to notate it as possible.

Lastly, unless the script includes extra pages at the end, such as a prop list, your last page of the script usually won't have a corresponding blank page to the right of it. If the script has a title page, I usually recycle this to the last page, so I have a blank side to scribble on. After all, there will probably be a lot of cues at the end of the show with lights down, so you will need somewhere to scribble notes. By now, you will realize that the advantage of inverting the script in this way is that none of my scribbles are on the printed text except the odd line across from specific words. This innovation allows me to eventually write up a cleaned-up version of the cues on the printed text side, undo my inversion of the pages and produce a clean cue script in a ring binder with the cues and the dialogue on the right for an operator to use or to archive[1].

What am I scribbling on these blank sides? Well, if you have followed my process up to this point, you will know that I have already developed my sound design in the sense of knowing what the purpose and meaning of each cue is as well as the different vocabularies of cues I will be using. I also know where I think these vocabularies of cues are to be used. So, I don't spend any effort in scribbling what I already know. Usually, what I don't know is where a long cue starts and where it ends so I make a note of these points with a continuing vertical line connecting them even across multiple blank sides if need be. Layered long sound cues use multiple vertical lines. For instance, a bed of birdsong and the sound of a car driving up. Each vertical line can have a different start point and end point. Also, I usually fill the pauses in the dialogue with sound. Since the pauses are often never in the same place after they have been through the preceding rehearsal process, I make a note of where they are now knowing that they may continue to change during tech and previews. Once I have designed cues to fill these pauses, it is easy to move them around when the pause moves.

As a result of my chosen level of design granularity, I usually build my beds using discrete elements instead of using prerecorded tracks or loops as previously explained. This means that I can trigger them to come in the pauses between the dialogue. I once sat in on tech of a student show that had used the sound of traffic close by. Unfortunately, since the traffic was a prerecorded long track that was looped, a lot of the passing cars passed at the same moment and competed with a very important bit of dialogue. The sound cue *stamped* on the dialogue. During tech, the director was constantly asking the student sound designer to reduce the volume to such a point that the traffic track ended up sounding like a mistake. The additional lesson here is that when we are asked for a change, we should make sure we know what the real need is so that the real issue can be fixed. The problem in this case was not overall volume but competing focus of attention. A clue is that if a director is continually asking you to reduce the volume of a sound cue to a point where it sounds like a mistake, then the cue is probably wrong in some way and needs to be rethought. Building loops from continuous uneventful beds overlaid by discrete attention competing elements that can be triggered independently in the gaps allows us to play the sound effects in what seems like a continuous loop so as not to *stamp* on any of the dialogue.

Most of the time during the designer run, we will be scribbling starting points and ending points as well as placing single cues, but we should also be on the lookout for new places where we can use elements from the vocabularies that we have already developed. An owl hoot here, a distant gunshot there. However, sometimes opportunities appear in the designer run that we have not anticipated at all for which we have no vocabulary. To give you an example, in *Cat on a Hot Tin Roof* by Tennessee Williams, for most of the play, what you see is what you get. Within this family that is continually fighting with each other, there are very few occasions where any of the characters are introspective and drop their guard. Yes, there is a surreal firework display going on outside that is in counterpoint to the dialogue inside the bedroom and yes, BIG DADDY makes a confession about being sexually propositioned by a child while on vacation, but neither of these revelations adds to your empathy for any of the characters. Yet there is a moment early on where MAGGIE almost does a soliloquy. *"Other men still want me…"*. Lost in her own thoughts while being ignored by BRICK, she talks about her early life and being a pageant queen. She lets her guard down and opens herself up. It is heartbreaking! So much so that it is worth picking out in a new light (literally) and underscoring with an emotion inducing musical underscore.

There is also a similar moment near the end of the show with BIG MAMA reminiscing about BRICK. *"Tonight, Brick looks like he used to when he was a little boy…"*. On both occasions, the characters seem to be standing outside of the current events and looking in on it as if from a different reality. I think I named the underscore loop I composed *Beauty*.

Telling really, as there is very little beauty in *Cat* as everyone is unrelentingly horrible to each other. I never identified these moments in the script or readthrough while working up my analysis and design, but they really became apparent during the designer run. So, I scribbled them down on the blank side opposite the dialogue.

As a designer, I have purposefully trained myself to be very fast in some parts of my process and very slow in others. For me, fast encourages adaptability and slow encourages in-depth granularization. It is a choice we as a designer can make for ourselves and deploy as necessary. I have already discussed how I granularize and slow down using the process of words to develop a design, but I also need to be agile and work fast when I am implementing my design. Designer runs go by fast. You may think that making a video recording of the run would be better than taking written notes, but Equity rules mean that every Equity participant would have to agree to it. In my experience, actors are happy to allow video recording for sections to help me when I need to build difficult cue sequences, but they are understandably reticent about capturing their performance of the whole show at the end of what was just the rehearsal room stage of their overall process. Additionally, video is time based and linear whereas scribbles on a page are presentation based and nonlinear. My scribbles allow me to be a lot more agile and fast.

We only get one shot at a designer run so we need to make it count. Set ourselves up with a process that allows us to be adaptable and work fast and glean all that can be gleaned. Giving ourselves a blank page on the right to scribble on beside each page of script on the left sounds so simple, yet we need to look at every part of our process, no matter how small and seemingly inconsequential, to make innovative changes for better outcomes.

Note

1 Instruct them to disregard any scribbles on the left as they are now not anchored to anything in the text.

Reference

Williams, T. (1955). *Cat on a Hot Tin Roof.* New York, NY: New Directions Books. pp. 49 and 156.

Next Morning   13

I purposefully don't work on anything to do with the show or its design after the designer run. I usually take the night off. This is another conscious design process choice we can make, when to work on our design and when not to. Sometimes, we need to give what we have a little time to unconsciously ferment inside of ourselves to allow connections and insights to be made. With experience, you will find other stages in your design process where rumination, as this unconscious fermentation is called, really pays off. It doesn't pay off everywhere, so we must really be attuned to where it produces insight and where it doesn't. I have found that points where my design gets major additions added to it such as the designer run are points where rumination usually pays off. Other points are…

- After initially getting the script and reading it.
- After the first design discussions after working up the script.
- After the meet & greet when a lot more contributions from others surface.
- After the first readthrough where characters start to come to life.

Like these other places, the designer run is like adding yeast to all the ingredients we have prepared so far. Now we just need to let the dough rest and rise before baking.

The day after the designer run is usually a day off for the cast. The Actors Equity Association is the union here in the United States that

DOI: 10.4324/9781003223160-13

represents actors and stage managers and contractually mandates the actors' day off. Most theatres usually try and arrange it so that tech isn't interrupted by an Equity Day Off, so in regional theatre, the day off is usually taken after the designer run[1]. This means we have a day to get our act together before tech starts.

Early next morning after the designer run, I start to integrate what I have learned from the run back into my *Narrative-Vocabulary-Purpose-Meaning* document. Purposes as well as meanings may need to be slightly updated or fleshed out further. This doesn't happen often as my design process has been rigorous up to this point, but placement usually changes, both the ins and outs of sound elements. Another thing that also seems to happen often is that additional opportunities unexpectedly appear where I can use some of the elements or ideas from the vocabularies I have already developed. Let me explain further.

All cues can be classified as either *Needs* or *Opportunities*. *Needs* as noted earlier are usually from stage directions or actor dialogue such as "Why is Amanda making such a loud noise!". On the other hand, *Opportunities* are what we also notice in the script that we believe will help reinforce or extend how we are telling the story. This is no different from what a scene designer does. The stage direction may only ask for a door through which a character enters, but a scene designer will usually contextualize it by putting that door in a wall and then use that as an opportunity to add bookcases and books and sconce lights and chintz curtains to flesh out the meaning or feeling of that room that has the door in it. This practice is so normal that we don't even register it as an opportunity having been taken. Since the opportunity usually reinforces the way we are telling the story, it follows that it usually consists of us just redeploying an element or idea that we have already developed. Designers spend a lot of time and creative thought developing the opportunities as the scripted needs are usually the bare minimum necessary for the dialogue to make sense. Remember, any new opportunities need always to be run through the *Narrative/Vocabulary/Purpose/Meaning* winnowing process, as already described, to make sure that they are real opportunities and not just our own ideas forced onto a script.

Design educators intrinsically understand the difference between what are classed as needs and what are classed as opportunities, even if they use their own design specialization-specific terminology. Students are usually started out identifying needs which are usually prescribed and therefore easy to identify. The students then develop some kind of design vocabulary they can deploy to fulfill these needs. They are then encouraged to find opportunities, other places that haven't been prescribed, where they can further use this vocabulary they have developed. Finally, they are encouraged to look for additional opportunities that will need additional vocabularies developing to fulfill. Each process necessarily follows the previous one and, in this book, I am obviously sharing my own detailed process for doing all of this. However, from an audience's point of view of experiencing a show, they have no idea what was a need or what was an opportunity. They are just cues or design elements. They all need to be called and they all need to be integrated into the show. To do this, we must now start interpreting our design as a set of instructions.

Most stage managers like to have their script marked up with cues before tech starts. To do this, first confirm with the stage manager how they would like to identify the cues. Usually, this will be a number beginning in a specific range, for example, lights start from #1 and sound starts from #500. There is nothing worse than for a lighting, sound and projections operator an hour into the show trying to quickly disentangle… *Lighting cue #117, sound cue #116, projection cue #117… GO!* There was a time when they wanted the sound cues to be letters to separate them from the lighting cues which were numbers. However, the amount of sound cues has increased significantly since those times. Another obvious reason to use numbers rather than letters is that it is easier to insert cues that get added in tech. Cue #117.5 is a lot more comprehensible than cue #YY.5 or even #YAa.

The start of a show is a very stressful time for everyone involved. It is a *nothing* to *something* moment; a zero to one moment. A lot is riding on getting it right night after night so we should be designing for this. Talking with our fellow designers at the designer run, we can usually get a feeling for how technically complex the start of the show is going to be. On these occasions, consider not starting at a multiple of 100 but somewhere in between. Stage managers like to be orderly about these kinds of things which is why the cues for the different departments usually start at multiples of 100, but in these situations, having an offset really helps. Think about listening to it in your headset… *stand by lighting cue #100, #100.7, #100.9, #101, 101.5, stand by sound cue #330, #330.5, #331, stand by projections cue #550, #551…. Go Lighting sound projections. Go lighting. Go lighting & sound. Go lighting, Go lighting sound projections.* This is a complicated sequence as it is and would probably be simplified further, but can you imagine if we all started at a similar starting number? Of course …, we don't want to offset the numbers such that we create the same problem of the similar numbers piling up for all the different departments at the end of the show as this is also another high-stress point now coupled with exhaustion. This is hard to predict in advance, so if it looks like it is going to happen, suggest jumping a block of cue numbers so that they don't all pile up.

Because of the need to get the information to the stage manager ASAP, I usually start an Excel spreadsheet of the sound cues so that I can immediately send it to them. I have seen a lot of different excel spreadsheets of sound cues over my career and in textbooks and I would say that they all have too much information in them. As designers, we must make a conscious choice where we keep all the information that we ourselves need to know as well as what we share and what we don't need to share with others. My *Narrative-Vocabulary-Purpose-Meaning* document is where I keep all the information that is not actual recorded sound, so the script and any excel spreadsheets are just tools used to communicate clearly with others and not anything more. A stage manager does not need to know where a sound cue is coming from to write it in their script and call it. Think about it, they are on headset behind glass listening to show monitor through some crappy mic that has probably remained undisturbed in the theatre for decades because it is rigged directly over the stage and hard to get to. Think about the information the Stage Manager needs at this point and clearly communicate it to them. Cue number is important. Page in the script is important and specific word in the dialogue or action on stage when the cue is to be called is important and also what everyone agrees the cue should be called is important. For a stage manager at this stage of marking up their script nothing else is important. Below is my day after designer run example from a production of *Cat on a Hot Tin Roof*. (Note that the annoying sound of the shower was eventually cut. The pretense being that at the top of the show BRICK was drying himself off having just showered.)

Cue	What	When
	Preshow Music	
	Music in house	
1	House Announce	
2	Top of Show Music revealing sound of shower	p. 17
3	Unmute and mute **Shower** Reverb	p. 17 and p. 18 with offstage lines

4	Shower out	p. 19 Visual?
5	Unmute and mute **Vom** Reverb	p. 18 Children Shriek Downstairs
6	Unmute and mute **Vom** Reverb	p. 24 Children yell below.
7	Croquet sounds	p. 30 Music is heard (no Croquet before this)
8	Croquet sounds	p. 30 MAGGIE "... lovemaking- strange- but **true**"
9	Croquet sounds	p. 31 MAGGIE "... I guess, as long as she **can**"
10	Croquet sounds	p. 31 MAGGIE "... drunk enough to believe **me**"
11	Croquet sounds	p. 32 BRICK "I've dropped my **crutch**"
12	Croquet sounds	p. 32 BRICK "[Hobbling out] '**Thanks**"
13	Croquet sounds	p. 32 MAGGIE "... walls in this house have **ears**"
14	Unmute and mute **Surround** Reverb	p. 36 for MAE's line outside the door
15	Unmute and mute **Vom** Reverb	p. 38 for offstage "Hey Mae" line
16	Unmute and mute **Vom** Reverb	p. 39 for "Wild Irish Rose" song off-stage (move later)
17	Unmute and mute **Surround** Reverb	p. 41 for BIG MAMA's lines outside door
18	Unmute and mute **Vom** Reverb	p. 43 for GOOPER shouting up the stairs
19	Unmute and mute **Shower** Reverb	p. 43 for BRICKS muffled answer from bathroom
20	Unmute and mute **Vom** Reverb	p. 44 for shouted goodbyes

Here are a couple of things to note. Since sound only had around 70 cues, the stage manager had already decided that sound would start at #1 (I think lighting started at #100). The words in bold in the **What** column are not where a cue comes from but the name of the mic channel that needs to be unmuted or muted. Since this show all happens in a bedroom, I added area mics and live reverb to any spoken dialogue from outside the bedroom. Also, for those of you who are familiar with the play, you will notice that cue #7 is listed in the stage directions as music from the garden. When developing the *Narrative-Vocabulary-Purpose-Meaning*, we realized that this cue has a similar purpose as the croquet sounds that follow it. Since we were about to also use music as underscore for MAGGIE's soliloquy as explained earlier, we decided to change it into another croquet sound cue since the music was not actually referred to in the dialogue[2]. To be honest, the thwack of a croquet ball is not something that is familiar to audiences these days especially here in the USA, so it was the accompanying reverbed voices of a family enjoying playing a game together outside which made these cues understandable in the context of the narrative.

Interestingly, it took me a while for my *Narrative/Vocabulary/Purpose/Meaning* process to make sense of the sounds from this game of croquet going on outside. In all the other Tennessee William's plays I have designed, I have always been impressed with his sophisticated use of sound. In *Night of the Iguana* for instance the character of SHANNON has a shouting match from afar with a bus full of tourists. SHANNON shouts words but the other end of the conversation is held up by pleading and abusive horn blasts from the bus. It really is very funny almost like a Harpo Marx gag. But in *Cat on a Hot Tin Roof*, the outside voices, music and croquet cues did not seem to me to be as sophisticated.

For a long time, the director and I could not understand the intended purpose of any of these cues. Yes, in simple terms, they provide a counterpoint of a family enjoying themselves outside while inside the bedroom MAGGIE and BRICK are fighting. The cues also force MAGGIE to close the blinds as she is undressing underlining a reoccurring theme in the play that MAGGIE and BRICK never have enough privacy to sort out their marital problems. But the placement of the cues did not seem to make any sense. Maggie does fleetingly acknowledge the game of croquet in her dialogue but that is only to talk about BRICK's detached way of playing sports. At first, we thought that it was just an aspect of all the sound cues being a bit cartoonish in this particular play. We put that down to Elia Kazan having had such a big influence in the writing and production of *Cat* unlike Williams' other plays. However, if we remove these outside cues completely to help define the *Purpose*, it didn't seem to make much difference. They essentially just interrupted a long monologue from MAGGIE.

After thinking about it for a while, I realized that was precisely the point. The monologue is about MAGGIE not being sexually fulfilled; something that would not be talked openly about and shared publicly by a woman in 1955. Remember, this is the era portrayed in the cinema when good married couples slept in individual beds and *nice* girls are not supposed to enjoy sex or even desire it (a very patriarchal view). Every section of dialogue between the cues is a step towards her broaching that subject. MAGGIE's every revelation in her monologue calls for a response from BRICK her husband, but he doesn't engage with her. So… essentially, MAGGIE just hears crickets (silence) after each attempt at broaching the subject and is forced to kick it up a notch and proceed on regardless. Also, realize that in 1955, some members of the audience would not be comfortable with hearing this subject even spoken about in a play, so for them, it also makes for a stairstep journey of acclimatization. It seems bizarre when you think about it, but these croquet cues are really the silence of BRICK refusing to engage with MAGGIE to sort out their marital problems.

There is an interesting thing about conveying silence in narrative. We usually describe silence using sound. "It was so quiet you could hear a pin drop". "'T'was the night before Christmas when all through the house. Not a creature was stirring, not even a mouse." A similar thing happens in theatre. Silence does not convey silence to an audience. Silence conveys *nothing*. To signify silence, we must use a signifier. A distant dog bark or a hoot of an owl or a gust of wind or the ticking of a clock, or even the scratching of an iguana. By inserting a sound that we would only hear if the world was silent, we can convey to an audience that it is quiet, that there is silence. That is why we say "crickets" when there is no response and only silence from someone who has been asked a question.

Notes

1 Off Broadway, Off-Off Broadway and Summer Season (and the UK equivalents) have different length tech and preview periods, so we schedule everything differently. However, all of them still try to maintain an uninterrupted process once we start tech to maintain the momentum before either first dress, first preview or some other milestone.

2 Subsequent dialogue does mention the children having sung and played piano, but not specifically at this point.

Reference

Williams, Tennessee. (2015). *Cat on a Hot Tin Roof*. Directed by Preston Lane, Greensboro, NC: Triad Stage, The Pearl Theatre.

Fade Ins and Outs 14

In the cue list in the previous chapter, the words in bold in the **When** column are the actual words in the dialogue that I as a designer want the cues called on. This is much more important than many designers realize. Like designers of lighting, projection and motion control, the sound designer's work is time-based. Sometimes, we think we can slip something in unnoticed, for instance, by fading it in slowly. But, at some point, the cue will be noticed, so we must ask ourselves when do we want the audience to notice it? Unfortunately, when fading something in slowly, each person will become aware of it at a slightly different level and consequently at a slightly different time. Perhaps we reason this is not a problem but be aware that any new stimulus commanding our attention takes a small but significant amount of time for a person to decode and process. We subconsciously must decide the value of any new stimulus and decide whether it *outranks* other stimuli. This processing takes both time and attention, with the unfortunate effect of keeping the audience member distracted from what may be crucial dialogue. Remember that this happens at a different level and therefore at a different time for each person, so we have no idea which members of the audience are missing which words in the script because their focus has been *stolen* by hearing a new sound cue. We as sound designers have now adversely impacted the intelligibility of the narrative. The result is that the production has potentially lost control of telling the story.

We may think that audiences can understand two things going on at the same time. They can… if neither of them is something new drawing

DOI: 10.4324/9781003223160-14

attention to itself. The reality is that humans cannot focus on two things at the same time. Yes, the two sides of the brain process what we are focusing on in two different ways[1], but it is still only the one thing we are focusing on. What really happens is that we humans continuously hop between the two or more things, checking in on each to make sure nothing new has happened that requires our full attention. The researchers call this continuous partial attention. With dialogue every word is new, meaning that your attention must be constantly checking in on it to make sure you are not missing anything. But it doesn't happen so much with the sound of waves lapping against a shore which are to some extent predictable. Consider that we call it *attention* – singular and not plural. There is no such thing as *attentions* or attending to more than one thing at any one time[2]. It is as erroneous as making a list of your priorities. Obviously, the highest one on the list is the priority, and the others aren't!

This *stealing of attention* is why sometimes actors who are in view but not engaged in the current action become distracting when they make up extraneous business for their character to do. This business steals the audiences' focus as it does not seem related to the current thrust of the narrative. In a film, they would just not be in shot. However, because they are in full view on stage, they feel their character needs to be authentic and they need to do something their character would likely do. I once watched a dress rehearsal of *Anna Christie* by Eugene O'Neill where a very moving scene between ANNA and her father, was completely upstaged by a brightly lit barman polishing drinking glasses that continually glinted and reflected the bright stage lights directly into our eyes blinding us. I understand that the director eventually dealt with this. However, it happens all the time.

In *Our Town* by Thornton Wilder, loved by high school drama departments, everything is mimed. This is great training for actors but is excruciating to sit through. While important dialogue is being delivered, other actors not involved in the focus of attention at that moment are continually stealing that attention by miming polishing their shoes or some other inane act. As a member of the audience, you are continually trying to figure out what they are miming and are not attentive to the dialogue at all. The experienced directors know how to deal with this and tone it down. Even just getting the characters to face away helps. These professional directors understand that they are not directing actors in a play so much as they are instead directing the audience's attention moment by moment.

Knowing all this, the way we achieve gentle fade-ins is to first establish them quickly at a low enough level so that everyone can be aware of them at the same time and then to fade them up to the desired level from there. To facilitate this, I have taught myself to use different clear language to describe each aspect of the level change. A fade-in (when sound is heard emerging from silence) is different from a fade-up (where sound is heard increasing in level) and a fade-down (where sound decreases in level but is still heard) is different from a fade-out (where sound gets quieter to a point of not being heard and is replaced by silence). Interestingly, fade-outs don't usually steal our attention the same way that fade-ins do unless the fade-outs are abrupt[3].

Evolution seems to have genetically primed us to hear the predators' paw snap the twig in the forest—something new needing our attention—rather than something that is already holding our attention gently fading out and not needing our attention anymore. In fact, rather than being aware of something slowly fading away, our focus is usually overtaken by something new needing our attention. Directors of Shakespeare plays intrinsically understand this and use it all the time. Two characters talk, they decide to do something and exit, and then a different set of characters enter talking about what they have just done or seen. There! Half of all Shakespeare scenes. Directors usually bring the second couple of characters on while the first is still exiting, even though neither of the pairs is supposed to be aware of the other pair. They do this so that the audience is not left watching something end but instead watch something else beginning; being overtaken by even more intrigue. This method of handing off the attention is far less soporific than watching characters exit a scene.

Another aspect to establishing a sound at a low but perceptible level first so that everyone is aware of it at the same time is to link that sound to a common event for the whole audience. Let me give you an example. In scene three of Tony Kushner's play *Angels in America: The Millennium Approaches*, LOUIS asks PRIOR why he is in a pissy mood and PRIOR rolls up his sleeve and shows LOUIS the lesion on his arm. Here is the dialogue from p27 of the TCG script.

PRIOR: *(He removes his jacket, rolls up his sleeve, shows Louis a dark-purple spot on the underside of his arm near the shoulder)*
"**See.**"
LOUIS: "That's just a burst blood vessel."
PRIOR: "Not according to the best medical authorities"
LOUIS: "What?"
(Pause)

"Tell me."
PRIOR: *"K.S., baby. Lesion number one. Lookit. The wine-dark kiss of the angel of death."*
LOUIS *(Very softly, holding Prior's arm)*: ***"Oh please…"***
PRIOR: *"I'm a lesionnaire. The Foreign Lesion. The American Lesion. Lesionnaire's disease."*

As you can see above, I have highlighted three separate words of this dialogue in bold. If we were to introduce an emotional musical underscore at this point in the play, it would have a different meaning depending on which of these three words the audience became aware of it. If they hear it on the word "See", it will underscore the lesion, the disease: AIDS. If the audience heard it on the words "Tell me", it would underscore LOUIS's concern for PRIOR. Lastly, if they heard it on "Oh please…", it would underscore PRIOR's concern for LOUIS. In essence, the underscore would stand in for either AIDS, LOUIS or PRIOR depending on where it was noticed and perceived to combine with the dialogue. These three cue points are only moments apart. Any slow fade in that hasn't been controlled when the audience will first perceive the underscore has the potential of the audience ascribing three completely different meanings to it. Once again, we will have lost control of the narrative.

The first time that we introduce emotional music underscore, it takes on one of these meanings which will then affect how we deploy this same underscore throughout the rest of the play. Rather than a character or situation owning the underscore, I usually talk about it as something that the underscore or sound *gets nailed to*. Not only does the underscore mean different things depending on what it gets nailed to, but that meaning now has repercussions to how the sound or underscore can be used in the rest of our design.

I use this a lot as a designer and my sound designs are peppered with underscores that I have nailed at that moment to some emotion or meaning being conveyed by the dialogue or the action. I then redeploy these underscores elsewhere in the show to add this same meaning or emotion to help manipulate the audience's perception and engagement with the story being told. The classic fun theatre sound example of this must be *The Woman in Black* adapted by Stephen Mallatratt from a novel by Susan Hill. Around 20 pages into the script, the WOMAN IN BLACK makes her first appearance half glimpsed in the darkness of the back of the house while KIPPS and JEROME are attending her funeral on stage.

I am obviously not the first sound designer to play a sub-bass frequency (felt rather than heard) to accompany her entrance. Once this WIB sound cue had been nailed to her appearance, the production had a lot of fun using it all over the place to imply that she was close and could appear at any moment, even when it wasn't written that she was meant to appear. We toyed mercilessly with the audience, and they thoroughly enjoyed it. We even used it after the curtain call during the walkout with some flickering lights to spook the audience one last time. Much of the time, however, this ability to nail a design element to a specific emotion or meaning gets used in far more serious and important ways.

This nailing and using of a design element is much more commonplace in the other design areas. It is probably easy for us to imagine that how a character first uses a set piece, or a prop can define its meaning. In *The Woman in Black*, a theatre soft goods hamper easily transforms into a pony and skip when required. Although it may be harder to imagine, the same thing can also happen with lighting. Writer Aaron Sorkin and director Thomas Schlamme used a very specific lighting design for the hallways that connected the offices in the White House in the series *The West Wing*[4] to give extra meaning to the upper torso *Walk and Talk*[5] shots they employed. As opposed to the more traditional flood lights for a hallway, the narrow spotlights spaced overhead meant that the walking (and talking) characters were constantly walking into and out of the light. Light, dark, light, dark. This constantly passing through this lighting effect accentuated the characters moving. This gave these scenes a fast pace to match the narrative. This was a dynamic White House always on the move dealing with crisis after crisis usually in the hallways. That very specific meaning got nailed to that kind of lighting and was then used in other locations elsewhere in the series when they needed to convey dealing with a crisis on the move.

In the spreadsheet, that I send the stage manager, I also hold some cue numbers if I do not know how all of us are going to accomplish something. In the same spreadsheet from above, below is the section that covers the fireworks sequence in *Cat*. This section is near the end of the show and obviously sound will have to coordinate with lighting. Although lighting will have an idea of what they are going to do, until we reach that part of the show in tech and try some things out as a design team, I will usually not know what the sound will need to support and contextualize. I usually save more cues than I think I will need just in case. It would really mess things up with the sequence of cues if I didn't have enough and the stage manager had to call many fractional cue numbers, especially during a complex sequence that needs to coordinate between production elements: lighting, sound, smoke/haze, pyro. So really, this spreadsheet is just reserving cues for me to use at certain points in the play. Basically, I am letting the stage manager know … you call this, and I will put something there but until we get to it in tech I have no idea what!

Cue	What	When
54	Saved for Fireworks	
55	Saved for Fireworks	
56	Saved for Fireworks	
57	Saved for Fireworks	
58	Saved for Fireworks	
59	Saved for Fireworks	
60	Saved for Fireworks	
61	Saved for Fireworks	
62	Saved for Fireworks	
63	Saved for Fireworks	
64	Saved for Fireworks	

Notes

1. As explained in the book *The Master and His Emissary* by Iain McGilcrist.
2. I can be argued that we can attend to words and music, two different things, at the same time such as in a song. But what is happening is that the words and music fuse into one in a kind of gestalt. If we played music that didn't go with the words, the fusing would not happen, and our attention would now be split.
3. Think of it as the absence of the sound fading in abruptly.
4. Although a TV series, it was very theatrically staged.
5. An explanation of the storytelling technique can be found at Wikipedia. Just look it up ☺.

References

Kushner, T. (2013). *Angels in America: Millennium Approaches* (Revised Edition). New York, NY: Theatre Communications Group. p. 27.

Mallatratt, S. & Hill, S. (1989). *The Woman in Black* (Acting Edition). London, UK: Samuel French.

O'Neill, Eugene. (2014). *Anna Christie*. Directed by Preston Lane. Greensboro, NC: Triad Stage, The Pearl Theatre.

The West Wing. (1999–2006). Created by Aaron Sorkin & Warner Bros. Television, NBC.

Wilder, T. (1938). *Our Town*. New York, NY: Coward-McCann.

Designer as Chef 15

Once I email this excel spreadsheet to the stage manager, I now start working with actual sounds. You are probably surprised that I have left making any sound to this late in the game, but if you have followed my design process this far, you will know that I do not construct any sound cues until I know exactly what I want to construct. I don't go looking for something. I imagine something and then I make it. I design something! As I explained earlier, I have worked hard over my career to really know my sound effects library, not as what it has been recorded as but as what it would sound like to an audience. Just as my *Narrative-Vocabulary-Purpose-Meaning* document has helped me construct in words a precise understanding of what a sound cue needs to accomplish, I can now use that definition to select and combine different sounds to make what I need. This is Designer as a chef, as in a kitchen!

At first, this seems impossible. My searchable sound library is upward of 100 gigabytes in recordings some of which I have recorded myself. But the problem is really no different from the English I speak. The Oxford English Dictionary has around 170,000 words in it and that doesn't include non-standard conjugations, inflections and jargon etc. Adding these brings the total up to over half a million words. However, it is not as daunting as you think because all those words are made from only around 15,000 unique phoneme syllables. More importantly, according to Robert Charles Lee[1], a published writer, 95% of everyday writing only uses about 3000 words and around 1000 words will suffice for 89% of your writing needs. Can you remember 1000 different sound elements and where to find them in your library? I can and you can too if you work

DOI: 10.4324/9781003223160-15

at it! I don't store them as a separate sound library, I just remember where to find them in my whole sound library as I would do any quote from a book in my real library. Remembering where to find them actually aids remembering them as you now have two things held in your memory: the sound and where to find it. This is important to me as I always build the cue from scratch and always go back to the original.

Sometimes I may need a slightly different bit from a particular recording to reflect the slightly different nuance I am wanting. Sometimes I may stumble across a sound file that I never took note of before because I didn't need it for anything and now it is exactly what I need. The process of going back to the original every time allows for this to happen. I make a significant amount of my sound cues from this group of very communicative sound elements and then add to it any *specials* that I need. If you think about it, this is no different from how a lighting designer designs. They have a basic plot that provides for most of their lighting cues and to that they add any specials they need.

The designer run was in fact the last piece of information that I needed before starting to build my cues. I now integrate that information back into my *Narrative-Vocabulary-Purpose-Meaning* document changing what needs to be changed and adding what needs to be added. From the vocabulary document, I now know exactly what I need to construct. For instance, these many dog barks for these many different dogs in these many different situations that make this overall journey when they are all put together.

This brings up something else to consider. If we never actually see the thing that is making sound in a show, the dog that is barking or the car that is approaching, that sound of the dog bark or car doesn't just stand in for the sound the dog or car makes, but it also stands in for the *actual* dog or car that is absent. The sound stands in for the *thing*, not just the sound that the *thing* makes. This is similar to the way that the two circular images on screen in a movie stand in for binoculars and are not the real format of the image we see when using binoculars[2]. It not only communicates that binoculars are being used but it also communicates what they are looking at. Similarly, our sound effect must communicate the actual *thing* and not just the sound the *thing* usually makes. It is this aspect that oftentimes trips up early career professionals and students sound designers. But it also sometimes trips up us experienced professionals.

For example, when *Miss Saigon* was first being mounted in the West End, there were all these stories making the rounds of how Andrew Bruce's sound team had worked with the Royal Air Force and used the new portable DAT tape recorders to record a helicopter. The idea was that they would have the cleanest recorded realistic sounds possible. This was at the start of my career when I was working in the sound department at the Royal National Theatre. One day we had a panicked visit from one of *Miss Saigon's* sound team requesting the helicopter sounds that we used. We had recently mounted a production of the kids show *Whale*, with sound designed by Christopher Shutt (of *Warhorse* fame), where a helicopter theoretically hovers over the stage and drops a ladder to the ice below. Christopher's helicopter built from a synthesizer patch was really convincing especially once gusting snowflakes and the implied shadow of the helicopter were added to the scene. So, we gave the *Miss Saigon* team our helicopter sound effect. I don't know if it ever got used in their production or not, but the whole episode did highlight the issue of mistaking the sound that the *thing* makes with the sound that is meant to stand in for the *thing*.

As an aside, have you ever listened to a helicopter up close? All you hear is the turbo fan engine. Since the sound of the *thwonk, thwonk, thwonk* of the blades are at such a low frequency[3] it takes quite a distance for the pressure wave the *thwonk* makes to become a sound that can be heard. Since we usually only experience helicopters from a distance, the *thwonk, thwonk, thwonk* sound of the rotating blades becomes the iconic sound. It is hard to record helicopters from this distance without picking up all the other environmental sounds, so it is very nearly impossible to record a sound that will convincingly stand in for a helicopter. Also, perfectly recorded reality misses the fundamental point of the theatre experience-that of providing a heightened version of reality. Sounds like the helicopter must be made. It must be designed. Christopher Shutt used a Roland synthesizer to make the iconic helicopter sound. That is why we as designers have a job!

One of the interesting things about designing sounds that represent the *thing* instead of the sounds that the *thing* makes is that you can also alter the sound effect to include any additional subtext of the *thing* you are wishing to communicate. We have already discussed this with the story of my students' opinion of the type of home, neighborhood, and family a particular front doorbell sound evokes. This consensus is from the point of view of the audience, but how can a designer use this? Let me use our trusty "dog bark" sound effect to demonstrate this. Since the audience never sees the dog, the dog bark not only stands in for the dog, but also stand in for what the dog is barking at. If a dog is barking happily, the person that is arriving outside is a nice person. If the dog is barking ferociously, the person arriving outside is a nasty person. So, the sound of the dog bark not only stands in for a dog, big, small, etc., but can also help characterize who the dog is barking at; nice, nasty, known, unknown. Couple that now with a specially chosen evocative sound of a doorbell that the person rings, then you have set up a tension between the new arrival and the other characters in the house, and you have done this all before the audience even sees who it is. That is why I am meticulous over my *Narrative-Vocabulary-Purpose-Meaning* document. I don't just need a dog barking; I need it to accomplish all these other necessary subtexts as well.

There is an old perennial British pantomime gag. A character knocks on the door and the character opening the door says, "You rang?".

I don't build every cue. I only build the first few cues we are going to get to in tech. The reason is that until we all see what the other designers and actors are contributing, and it all gets put together in the space, I don't really know how our production is telling the story. For show after show during my career, I have noticed that it takes us tech-ing a couple of scenes for everyone to get a sense of what it is we have in front of us. When we start tech, the designers of elements that can adapt and respond to each other are all noticing what the others are bringing to the table and therefore changing what we are doing in response. So, design-wise, the start of tech is usually very fluid. You are adjusting to others who in turn are adjusting to you. It all needs time to settle down so that we all get a sense of what it is we have in front of us, what direction we are heading in and how all the creative elements of our production are coalescing together to tell the story.

There has been an evolution of the way I design. With show after show, I noticed that the scenes we teched at the start, nearly always had to be comprehensively re-teched and drastically changed when we came back to them. It was as if we hadn't really decided yet how we wanted them to work. Remember I discussed earlier how the script is a complex intricate mechanism that represents the way the story is being told? We designers are also building our own complex exoskeleton on the top of this script mechanism to help tell the story to the audience. We must wait for enough of the parts of this composite mechanism to be in place before we can see it for what it is and can then add to it appropriately. I now design with that in mind. My first cues are just showing everyone what I have developed and can bring to the production and how adaptable I can be. After all, the more adaptable you are, the more your cue survives and makes it into the final production, the more accolades are bestowed upon you (well… seldom the last bit!).

Some directors like to start tech-ing the show not at the top of the show but with the scene or part of the show that they think is going to be the most technically challenging. The idea is that if we sort out the issues while we are all fresh, when we get to it in tech, we will have already sorted it out and it won't bog us down. In my experience, it seldom turns out this way for the very reason that if we tech this difficult section first we still haven't had the benefit of the learning process (explained above) and may end up on the wrong track. By the time we get to it the second time around as we tech through the show in sequence, we know a lot more about how we are making our show work, so we usually must throw out much of our earlier effort. This makes working out-of-sequence in this way less of an advantage than first imagined. But this does bring up a good point. If you are only building the first few cues for the start of tech, do find out what part of the show you are starting with.

Some directors also like to *Dry-Tech* or *Cue-to-Cue* their shows before the actors arrive for tech. A *Dry-Tech* is where we go through the whole show listening to and looking at the cues from lighting, sound, projections, MoCo and the changing of set elements and props—or any combination of these that they want to tech. This usually doesn't involve costume as this would not make any sense without the actors being there wearing them. A *Cue-to-Cue* is like a *Dry-Tech* but is usually just a single design area such as sound or lighting. The idea is that if we can get it all sorted out beforehand, nothing will hold up tech-ing the show when we add actors. In my experience, this has the same issues as just tech-ing the difficult bits first. The design elements that can adapt at this stage respond not just to each other as explained earlier but also to what the actors are doing and the lines they are speaking. Their actions and the voices are also part of that additional mechanism that needs to come fully into view before we can all confidently move forward. As a result, because it is missing these key elements, anything that is dry-tech'ed usually needs further adjusting when the actors are added back in during the *real* tech. Also, because dry-techs go through the show very quickly in comparison to a real tech, there is little time for each design element to respond to each other.

In my personal experience in the case of sound design, any levels that are set in a quiet theatre without actor voices always need adjusting once the real tech starts. Lighting also usually has issues because although they often use *walkers*—people who stand in for where the actors will stand on stage—they are not moving into and out of those positions in the same way the actors would. As a result, for lighting, sound and projections, the timings of cues will all need adjusting when the actors are added. Still, tech, when all the other production elements get added, is a very stressful time for directors. It must be like you are juggling and suddenly ten more balls get added to the ones you are already juggling. Dry tech gives directors a chance to practice with those extra balls before they get thrown into the mix, so for them, it may be beneficial.

Notes

1 https://www.quora.com/How-many-words-are-in-the-average-English-speakers-working-vocabulary
2 Of course … in a movie, we will probably also see the binoculars at some point, whereas in theatre sound, we never see the dog or the car.
3 Not to be confused with its speed of rotation.

References

Holman, David. (1989). *Whale*. Directed by Tim Supple. London, UK: Royal National Theatre, Lyttleton Theatre.

Morpurgo, Michael & Stafford, Nick (adapter). (2007). *Warhorse*. Directed by Marianne Elliott & Tom Morris. London, UK: Royal National Theatre, Olivier Theatre.

Schönberg, Claude-Michel & Boublil, Alain. (1989). *Miss Saigon*. Directed by Nicholas Hytner & Cameron Mackintosh. London, UK: Theatre Royal Drury Lane.

16 Content, Distribution, Environment

This need for fast adaptability caused me over the years to rethink my design implementation process. The way I now build my cues is by thinking of them in terms of *content, distribution* and *environment*. Let me explain. The content is obvious. These are the sounds or the music or the live reinforced cues I will be using. The distribution is where all those sounds come from and how they combine in the theatre space as perceived by an audience. I remember the Sound Designer Paul Groothuis telling me a long time ago that he initially plays his sound cues from every loudspeaker and then walks around the theatre deciding which loudspeakers he doesn't want the sound to come from. This is a *take away what you don't want* subtractive approach instead of the more usual *add what you do want* additive approach. This concept was originally used by the early analogue synthesizers that used either additive or subtractive synthesis. The unique sounds they made were either made by adding pure tones together or starting with noise and filtering out what aspects of the noise they didn't want. Each approach works and is a valid process depending on your design situation.

In my own process, I take this distribution approach one step further. Since I use many sounds to construct each sound effect, the individual sounds don't all have to come from the same loudspeaker. They can be distributed around the theatre, playing each individual element of my sound cue out of a different loudspeaker, creating a kind of lifelike immersion for the audience. This allows me to swap around which sound is coming out of each loudspeaker to make it *read* more convincingly to an audience. It also means that I can delay or advance each individual sound element in time with respect to the whole thing to further shape it if necessary.

I often have a single element start before the other elements are added and I often fade out elements one by one before then fading out the whole thing completely. It's a similar concept to when painters *feather* one color into another or when watercolorists use a *wash* to make a gradual transition between two colors. This makes for a powerful level of adaptability of each cue. The net effect of this in three-dimensional theatre is that the whole sound cue now has a sense of three-dimensional movement associated with it and can *hug* the performance more closely. For example, for the top of the show music cue, fading out the individual sound elements in the seating section before fading out the ones up stage will have the effect of helping the audience get settled and direct their attention to the scene starting onstage.

This sequencing of individual elements is no different from what a director does all the time. If you watch directors in tech, they are continually trying out different sequencing of moving characters to clarify the group body language of all the actors on the stage so that it hugs the unfolding story more closely. Also, if you watch them choreograph a scene change or transition that an audience will see, they are usually very specific about the sequence of when pieces of scenery go off or come on. This is important to them in clarifying the flow of the transition; the flow of leaving one scene and ending up in a different scene with an audience watching. Some scenes are very powerful, and the transition is choreographed to help the audience linger on the scene that has just ended. At other times, the transition immediately breaks with the last scene, so as to communicate moving on. These are choices that need to be made. Once you add time to the other three dimensions, the flow becomes an element that can and should be designed.

This concept of distribution is no different from how a lighting designer uses *magic sheets*. Whereas a lighting plot is the position and circuit of all the lighting instruments in a theatre, a magic sheet details what each lighting channel achieves on the stage (or in the house). Their use is very personal to each lighting designer and there is no set standard. Although these magic sheets take many forms, they provide a *cheat sheet* that allows a lighting designer to conceptually group[1] far-flung lighting instruments together to achieve a specific look or a sequence of looks. It allows the lighting designer to think of their content and control it in a different way. Like my distributions, these same conceptual groupings tend to be used repeatedly as the lighting designer works through the show.

I remember one time I was forced to quickly re-content a distribution template in front of the actors during tech. I had built several three-dimensional immersive soundscapes to follow the different scene locations and the different times of the day. I also used slow crossfades between them to speed up time and seamlessly transition between afternoon to evening over a period of more than half an hour. While we were tech-ing, I realized that I needed another different immersive soundscape to crossfade to in between, so I asked the director if I could take five minutes on stage to quickly construct one in the space. I went on stage and got my assistant to play the template I had already set up. I then quickly repositioned each sound, "swap the frogs from that loudspeaker with the wind from this loudspeaker" etc. I then rebalanced the whole thing "Frogs up 3dB. Wind down 6dB" etc. The process was very fast and decisive, and it only took a couple of minutes out of the tech. When I had finished, a couple of the actors who had sat there watching the process, came up to me afterward and said that they had never understood what it was that a sound designer did, and now they do. Of course, I usually do this work beforehand, so no one is ever aware of it. They usually only hear the resultant sound effect. Like everything else in the theatre, it is hard to understand how magic is made if all you get to witness is the end result.

Turning now to the last of the three, environment. With every individual sound I use, I also generate and record a stereo reverb track of that sound that is 100% *wet* with no original *dry* sound in it. This means that each sound cue is now three tracks: the original sound, left reverb and right reverb. I always place the reverb in opposite loudspeakers to where I have placed the sound effect. Think of it as a triangle. One corner is the original *dry* sound element, and the other two corners are the left and right *wet* reverbs. I play the reverb just loud enough to give a sense of an aural environment that is different from that of the actual theatre space. After all, we have a real theatre but what we don't have is an environment that realistically (or stylistically) represents the place we are trying to recreate within our suspension of disbelief. The net effect is that each sound element with its attached reverbed tracks feels like it now sits within a three-dimensional environment which is closer to how we experience the real world. This then adds a level of heightened authenticity to the sound element. Now add to that the fact that I do this for all the individual sound elements that make up that sound cue and you will soon realize that each loudspeaker is potentially playing a dry sound element as well as also playing numerous additional reverb tracks from other sound elements that are playing in the other loudspeakers. It sounds complicated but it really isn't in practice.

In the same way that the dog bark stands in for the actual dog, the reverb stands in for the environment and not just the sound that the environment makes. These environments are seldom real spaces, but they are always manipulatively emotional. For me, theatre is a three-dimensional experience unfolding over time, so like the set, costumes and lighting, I want my sound to mimic this three-dimensional experience changing over time, even if it is just a single dog barking in the distance.

Once I reconceptualized the implementation of my design process into content, distribution and environment, I realized that it was mainly the content that changed from cue to cue. I would end up using the same distributions over and over again just repopulating them with different content. So, I made these same distributions into a template that I could just copy and use again and again. Interestingly, I noticed that the number of these different distribution templates loosely followed the number of different vocabularies I had developed, although not always. I also noticed that my environments would seldom change once I had chosen the specific reverb that I would use for the sounds the characters hear and the sounds they don't hear.

Now that I had the distribution templates tweaked in the actual theatre to sound how I wanted them to sound to an audience, next I would make sure each piece of content had associated environments prepared at the same volume and in the same format so that they would fit correctly into a template. This meant that my replacement cues would work out of the box the first time without having to first listen to them in the space. The levels would still need some fine adjustment, but it was not horrible. A simple way to understand this is to think of each sound cue as just a candy (sweet) wrapper. I could replace the actual candy inside each wrapper if I made that candy of the same shape and size. The vending machine would now dispense the candy just the same as it did before, but this time the taste inside would be different—the sound content would be different. I would not have to build a different dispensing machine for each new candy—or sound cue—I came up with.

Not only has this conceptual and physical splitting up of my design helped speed up my process of implementation, it has also allowed me to only have to build a couple of cues in front of where we are in the tech process. It is this speed and replacement ability that has allowed me to collaborate more fully with my fellow designers, the actors and the director. I can see how our telling of the story is shaping up moment by moment and pull into the *wrappers* just the right sounds so that my next cue advances the shape of the narrative that we are all creating. It also allows me to aurally support aspects of the other design elements as well as take advantage of gaps in the *aesthetic bandwidth*[2] that have opened up. I believe that part of being a collaborative designer is to support the work of the other creatives and make their contributions better in whatever way I can. I can only do this if I can see where things are heading and if I am adaptable enough and fast enough to respond.

On a personal note, as a designer, I now luxuriate in only having a couple of cues built in front of where we are in the tech process. I used to really stress about not having everything complete and perfect for the start of tech. It took me years to realize that the whole reason we have a tech/dress/preview process that goes on for days and sometimes weeks or months is that it only must be perfect at the end of that process not at the start. At the start of tech, the cue just has to be good enough that everyone understands what it is attempting to achieve so that they can assess if they want to keep it or not, also so that they can respond to it and integrate it into the direction of their own creative process. Bottom line… the cue only needs to be good enough not to get cut.

There is also something exciting about always being on the verge of running out of cues. It must be like walking a tightrope (though I have never tried). There is this concept that the most creativity happens at the boundary between too much and too little structure. It is known as the edge of chaos theory. Too much structure makes something too fixed and hard to change. Too little structure and any change, although much easier, cannot be supported and sustained, and therefore, quickly collapses. Because I have trained myself to be fast and adaptable, I now purposefully adjust my process such that I am always working at this creative edge of chaos.

The way I have divided up how I implement my own design process using content, distribution and environment may not be suitable for your design process, but something else like it may work. Look for it. Observe your implementation process, see how it is constructed, see which parts change a lot and which parts change less often. Reconstruct it such that more of your time and creativity is applied to the part that changes more often and less of your time is spent on the parts that seldom change. Innovate a quicker better design process for yourself. Become more agile and adaptable so that you can collaborate better.

Notes

1 This is different to physically programming the different channels on a lighting board into a group, although this may also happen.
2 For an explanation of Aesthetic Bandwidth see my paper of the same title on the USITT Sound – Research in Sound website. https://www.usitt-sound.org/2019/03/21/aesthetic-bandwidth/

Quiet Time   17

For me, the next thing that happens is quiet time. In fact, I try to schedule two quiet times. The first quiet time is a *system quiet time* and can be scheduled any time after the system is rigged and functioning. This allows for time to fix any major system or rigging issues that arise before the second, *design quiet time*.

Since I am usually resident at the theatre leading up to the weekend of designer run, the *system quiet time* usually takes place a day or two before the run. In this system quiet time, I listen to every element of the system making sure that a sound can be routed to each loudspeaker and that we all agree on what that loudspeaker is to be called. If channel #1 goes to the down stage left D/S/L loudspeaker, then I need to confirm that is indeed what is happening by making sure that sound is only going through that one channel and not any other, and that the sound is emerging from that one loudspeaker and no other. This may sound obvious, but I cannot tell you how many times, as a guest designer, I have routed an effect to a loudspeaker on the left and it comes out of the right one instead. This is not usually incompetence; it is because sound operators mostly sit *front of house* FOH behind the audience, so they usually think of things from house directions and not from stage direction. From their perspective stage right S/R is house left, etc. Also, the operators during my career mostly being western in culture, they like their mixing desk to be set up from left to right; the leftmost output is the leftmost loudspeaker which would be labeled D/S/R which feels like a mistake.

During this system quiet time, I also listen to the noise floor, for hums and buzzes, and I also listen for dynamic range. Can I get a sound as loud

DOI: 10.4324/9781003223160-17

as I want it to without clipping and distorting and does it also still retain detail when driven very quietly? If there are any system fidelity issues, they need to be dealt with and fixed before they *eat* into the second quiet time which should be all about the design and nothing to do with the system.

I used to just schedule to use only one quiet time but for show after show, I realized that half of this precious design quiet time was taken up fixing sound system issues and not implementing the design. A separate system quiet time can be scheduled when others are also working in the theatre. The other departments can usually be warned and stay quiet when required. In truth, most of the system quiet time is spent not playing anything loud in the space but troubleshooting, tracing signals and swapping out cables. None of these tasks require a quiet theatre so other departments can continue to work as they need. This was an easy innovation of my process for me to make once it became clear to me.

I try to schedule the second quiet time, the *design quiet time*, the night after designer run so I have some time to integrate what I have learned from the run and prepare some sounds. This is also the night before the start of tech in regional theatre in the USA, so there are usually many departments vying for extra time to finish their work before tech starts. As you can imagine in these hours before the tech starts, it is very difficult to get time in a theatre that is quiet enough without lighting clanking around with a Genie lift (cherry picker) or stage crew sawing or worse… angle grinding something. After years of not being popular at production scheduling meetings because of insisting no one else be in the theatre with me during my design quiet time, I have found an innovation that has worked well for my process. Paints! After the stage crew and lighting eventually go home the night before tech, the paint on the stage usually must be touched up before the start of tech the next day so the paint crew descend and start painting.

I have really grown to love the paint crew over my career. In my opinion, these are the unsung heroines and heroes of the theatre. They are all such interesting, enigmatic, talented people. Theatre people tend to be a bit homogenous as a group, but paints are like a breath of fresh air from a different creative universe. They work quietly and methodically with incredible detail and artistry. Art on demand! Enigmatic magic making or *Enigmagic* as I like to call it.

With a little bit of negotiation beforehand, I can usually get paints to agree that I and my crew can join them during their touch-up time the night before. They are usually amenable to not playing any music while painting, and I can usually assure them that I will turn on any fans needed to dry the paint once our quiet time is done if they leave before we do. Because anyone stepping on wet paint is *verboten* in theatre, everyone else stays away when paints are on deck and apart from the odd creak of a ladder being moved, it is wonderfully quiet with the added benefit of being under work lights and not pitch-black. I do make sure that if I am about to play a loud sound, no one is up a ladder, and I also announce it before I play any sounds—*Loud sounds in the house!* Coordinating with paints has changed recently as the ubiquitous cell phone conversations are starting to invade this quiet time. There will come a time when asking them to only text will not work for them, and I will have to innovate again. But I like innovating. I have done it all my life.

Designer quiet time is when I build the distribution templates that I am going to use. I build one for sounds from different locations outside. I build another for sound cues we hear and don't see such as dogs barking etc., and yet another for the practical sound cues that we hear and see, such as a telephone or practical radio etc. As well as realistic sound cues, some of them are also emotional. I build templates for emotional underscores and for the top-of-show and scene change music. As I said earlier, the number of different distribution templates I need usually closely tracks the number of different vocabularies I have in my *Narrative-Vocabulary-Purpose-Meaning* document. I usually build each template and then populate it with the content needed when that template is first used.

I know the template will need adjusting once all the other elements are added in tech and we all learn how our production is telling the story. Until I have the template working the way that will fit the show, I don't want to populate it with any more content for the additional cues. Sometimes, the template is not large enough and needs more channels and loudspeakers to get the effect I am looking for or at other times it is too large and needs trimming down to be more focused. Interestingly, this varies more with what lighting and acting is doing than any other production elements, so I usually must wait for tech to start to finetune this aspect. Lighting and acting define the size of the world that we as an audience pay attention to and therefore defines the size that the sound environment needs to support. Sometimes as this attention size gets bigger, my supporting sound environment also gets bigger, and at other times, it's the other way around and sound's contribution is designed so as not to compete with the size of the audience attention. I never know until I see it all in front of me.

Additionally, the nucleus of the direction that the sound is emanating from is sometimes not where I had thought it would be. Also, as discussed earlier, what kind of content I thought would be good coming out of one loudspeaker needs to be moved to another loudspeaker to work better. Lastly, the balance and levels will need changing once we add the actor voices and noise floor of their movement. Once the templates have been adjusted for all these factors and are how I want them to be, I can then go ahead and use them repeatedly, repopulating them for additional cues.

But for now, all I am trying to achieve in my design quiet time is to get a starting point for all my templates and to teach my sound team how the templates can be quickly adapted to accommodate what we learn along the way. So, after all that is done, I turn on all the fans to dry the stage and we all head to our beds in preparation for the start of tech the next day.

Tech

18

The day of tech dawns. This is going to be a long, exciting and stressful day. Because the previous night was a long one, I usually have a leisurely morning and don't go anywhere near the theatre until mid-morning if tech starts at noon. There was a time when I used to go into the theatre early, but I realized that there is nothing I could do. I couldn't play any sound because there was so much noise in the theatre as the stage crew usually had music blasting to accompany them working. Even when stage management starts to bring some order to the chaos on stage in preparation for the arrival of the actors, the cacophony from the stage crew is usually replaced by the sound of incessant vacuuming. Because of this, I have ditched all my high-end headphones and replaced them with over-the-ear noise-cancelling headphones. Sadly, these are not the greatest fidelity (usually upper base heavy) but at least now I can hear if I need to edit a sound file on my laptop while the vacuuming is happening[1].

Over the years, I have taken to meeting with my team instead. We usually meet somewhere off-site for coffee before tech starts. As a designer, I am also designing our team dynamics to meet the challenge of tech, and team building is an important aspect of my design process. Designs are delivered by teams!

I made a mistake once which has stayed with me for the rest of my career. In the heat of the moment, I *chewed out* a house sound person when I realized that what I wanted to play out of a loudspeaker in the left seemed to be coming from the right instead. It turned out that I was wrong as it was a reflection I was hearing. However, my frustration caused me to lose a team member. Even though they remained on the

DOI: 10.4324/9781003223160-18

show and continued to work very professionally, they were never on my side after that point. They felt bad and I felt bad. It also upset the rest of the team who felt forced to take sides which just exacerbated the situation. The needless friction it added couldn't help but affect the design. I learned that day that if they are not on your side, you don't have a team!

After stage management has retaken the stage and ejected the stage crew, I usually take a walk around to make sure that no cables have been damaged or interfered with and that any loudspeakers within striking distance are still pointing in the original direction I set them. There are always going to be issues, it is the nature of the beast. They just need to be identified and fixed before the problem happens and everyone else is aware of it, so I have taught myself to be very vigilant in the minutes before tech starts and personally check absolutely everything.

So… tech finally starts. The actors have done their walk through with stage management who have shown them their entrances, exits, crossovers and props tables etc., and everyone has set up their opening salvo of cues. Almost immediately after "house lights down…", these first cues get stopped, various things get adjusted and we go through the sequence again. Let's look at this in detail.

Because this is the first time that all the elements (except costumes) are being brought together, we are all realizing that what we thought our combined product would be doing is slightly different than we had imagined. Timings are different, sequences are different, the shape of the transition into the show is different, the area that we want an audience to be focused on instant by instant is different, the relative balance between the different design elements is also different. So, we stop, and those design elements that can, adjust so that our contribution will fit in better with everyone else's contributions. Then we go through these first cues again. Once again even though this time we usually get a little further into the show, it gets stopped again. We make further adjustments, and we go through these first cues yet again. This is so common an occurrence as to be unremarkable, but let's try and understand what is happening here because it offers some opportunities for innovating our design process.

Our first design process question should be, why didn't it work perfectly the first time? As alluded to above, when we design anything, we try and imagine how it will fit in with all the other design and acting elements. We imagine a kind of overall *aesthetic context* that includes all the other elements apart from our own and we design our own element to fit in with and support this imagined context. Every designer, actor and director is doing this as we are building our own design element or character or show. Yes, there are some *known knowns* to use the infamous phrase. We are all working from the same script, and each actor and the director has witnessed what the other actors are doing during rehearsals. We all have also seen concrete design proposals from sets and costumes as discussed earlier. However, the rest is a *known unknown* meaning that we really don't know what the contribution of each design areas is going to be like. We think we know, but there is always going to be a slight disconnect between what we imagined their design would be and what they actually produce.

But being a known unknown, we *do know* that we don't know and therein lies the power. Rather than waste time trying to predict this aesthetic context more accurately, the time is better spent making sure we have built some adaptability into our process and product. There is a great book, *Fooled by Randomness* by Nassim Nicholas Taleb[2]. The premise of this book is that instead of trying to predict random events which (by definition) is impossible, we should instead be building resiliency into our systems to accommodate for that randomness. We should be building a level of what I like to think of as *just-in-time-adaptability* into our designs. This is not just an aspiration. We need to think about how we can purposefully build adaptability into our design process and our product in such a way that it can be executed quickly.

Let me give you an example. Costume designers (and the costume department) always leave extra fabric at the seams in case the costume must be taken in or let out. They are designing leeway into their design. Even after they have fitted a costume to an actor, they do not know if they will need to let it out or take it in or by how much. It is essentially random depending on how the actor moves or how easily they can get into or out of the costume as well as a whole slew of other reasons such as suddenly having to accommodate a mic pack or a safety harness because they are leaning over the edge of the pit. Also, some actors change size and shape when they inhabit a character. I operated the sound for a production of *A View from the Bridge* by Arthur Miller directed by Alan Ayckbourn with the sound designed by Rob Barnard when I was at the Royal National Theatre in 1987. The character EDDIE CARBONE was played by Sir Michael Gambon. The costume designer Lindy Hemming would tell the story that Gambon physically changed his shape when he inhabited his character such that they had to continually let out his costume. As the show was in the old Cottesloe Theatre, I would pass him while he was warming up in the internal drum road[3] before every show. I knew not to acknowledge him or distract him, but I would witness him physically changing into this longshoreman. His chest became enormous, and he would move in this very un-Michael like way. Fittings were useless with Michael unless he was in character. The lesson learned is that what we do have control over is if our design can accommodate these eventualities and if we can build this adaptability into our design process.

When I first started out in sound, most sound cues were played off tape, either reel to reel or NAB cartridge (cart). This meant that any change that was needed, over and above when the sound was cued and how loud it was, would have to wait until the next day. In those days, we spent our nights rerecording, redubbing, remixing, reloading carts and reassembling reel to reel sequences so that we were ready to play the new updated sound cues the next day. Sound's inability to adapt quickly was seen by everyone else as a needless friction to the creative process and made for miserable long nights for us sound designers. Sound is now computer based, so we can now adapt very quickly. *"Waiting for sound"* is a thing of the past! The technology has changed for the better, but can we also change our design process for the better?

As we have discussed earlier, recognizing, or implementing a structure such as content, distribution and environment helps better target the parts that do change and leaves intact the parts that seldom change. Not wasting time recreating the parts that seldom change and only focusing on the parts that do change makes you faster at adapting. Also, if you can, not having to privately confirm your change before throwing it out there for all to see/hear cuts out an unnecessary step. For sound, this means that if I record and format all the cues in a similar way, I don't have to listen to them in the space first before I use them in a new cue as we move forward. These cues are good enough to be immediately thrown into the tech process without bringing the tech to a grinding halt. This saves me time.

The salient issue here is that your process of adaptability needs to produce a product that is just good enough so as not to stop tech. This is a particular issue projection has at this point in its evolution. In my experience, throwing rough projection cues into tech tends to stop the tech dead in its tracks. It's an interesting phenomenon that is too big to delve into here, however, it will improve as the technology becomes more robust and the designers develop their own processes of adaptation. It reminds me of the early days of using samplers for sound in theatre. We did amazingly creative things, but it was also a big hot mess a lot of the time that tended to bring tech to a grinding halt. Interestingly, stopping tech happens a lot with costumes. Any slight costume issue always seems to stop the tech. Firstly, this is because it directly impacts that actor, but it is also because costumes usually do not appear on stage until first dress rehearsal. This means that they do not have the same amount of time as the other design elements to get it right before the first preview. Have a kind thought for costume designers. They are delivering twice as much in half the time!

Another way to speed up our changes and make us more adaptable is to clearly see the process that we all are engaged in, its ebb and its flow. There is a lot of down time while tech is stuck fixing something and you will always see the other professional designers use this *stuck time* to adjust whatever they need to adjust so that they themselves never have to hold up the tech. Lights get refocused, set pieces get moved, props get swapped out and costumes get a quick stitch or a safety pin. It's like a pit stop in a formula one race. Everyone knows exactly what they need to do and then Bam! They do it and we are back into tech. As a sound designer, I also use this *stuck time* to push forward with populating my templates to build the next slew of cues.

As you can see, speed and adaptability are not about doing less, it is more about…

- Recognizing where the changes happen in your design implementation structure/process.
- Focusing your process of adaptability to happen at those places.
- Recognizing the points in the overall tech process where changes can happen without further holding up the process.
- Taking advantage of them.
- Recognizing the ebb and flow of tech and taking advantage of *stuck time* to make changes.

But there is a situation where you do have to limit your adaptability. Everyone knows what feedback is. It is caused when the sound from the loudspeaker gets back into the microphone and is then reproduced by the loudspeaker only to be picked up yet again by the microphone. The cycle occurs repeatedly ad infinitum in a feedback loop. Very quickly you have a screaming sound system. What you probably don't know is that one way to stop feedback is to introduce a short delay into the signal such that the sound is *held up* very slightly before it exits the loudspeaker. This delay partially breaks the cycle. The delay can be so short that it isn't noticeable but it can substantially reduce the feedback. What you may also not be aware of is that there is another feedback loop happening during tech. Our process of adapting is a feedback loop. When tech stops and we adapt our own contribution to fit in with what we have seen and heard the others do, we are always fitting in with the last iteration and not the iteration that is about to happen. The other designers have now also adapted their contribution to fit in with us and with everyone else. Everyone has moved forward (including you) but everyone is now adjusting to something that was *then* and is not *now*. Adjusting to the others is a kind of feedback, but now the delay of always being one step behind is a problem rather than helping.

This kind of delay and the problems it causes is well understood in the field of systems thinking[4] which views everything in terms of inflows, stocks and outflows. Inflows and outflows regulate the flow like a water faucet or tap does and stocks are a resource like the amount of water in a bathtub. The inflows and outflows can be controlled using information from the stock, i.e., when the bath gets too full (the information) the outflow tap gets increased (the control), or the inflow tap gets decreased so that the bath doesn't overflow. The flow can also be controlled by information from another flow, i.e., if the input tap gets increased the output tap also gets increased so that the inflow is equal to or less than the outflow and the bath doesn't overflow. This information and these controls are the feedback loops that either bring a system back into balance or reinforce an aspect, depending on the goal that is needing to be achieved. In our example, the bath remains full but not overflowing. People who think in systems break down the whole world from politics to population growth into these simple systems. They show that problems arise when either a flow is being controlled in the wrong direction or by the wrong information or when there is a delay in the control somewhere so that the system is always overreacting and always needs further correcting.

Our problem of adapting in tech is essentially that of a delay which causes us to overreact. We are adjusting for something that happened in the past and not the present. In systems thinking terms this produces oscillations, cycling between overcompensating and then having to correct and overcompensate in the opposite direction. The system thinking solution to oscillations is called damping. Damping is, never fully adapting in the first place or purposefully under adapting so that you don't overshoot. For us designers, the best way to approach this is to assess what we did; our contribution the last time tech was stopped. Figure out what we would like to do and then only go partway there. It sounds counterintuitive at first and indeed while we are getting used to working in this way it may be a bit messy. But if we persevere, we will eventually get the hang of it and be fully in control of this high-level adaptation that we are applying to our own process of adapting.

These stops and starts happen continually throughout the tech process, so any effort we put into making sure both our product and our process remain adaptable will pay off handsomely throughout our career.

Notes

1 Once played a loud looped sound of a vacuum cleaner in the theatre for half an hour as a joke during this period and no one batted an eyelid!
2 I believe it is a better book than his more famous *Black Swan*.
3 There is a secret roadway that runs through the bowels of the Royal National Theatre building that allows a 18 wheeler (pantechnican) to unload at the dock of each theatre.
4 An excellent primer is *Thinking in Systems* by Donella (Dana) Meadows. Look for free pdf on the internet.

References

Meadows, D. (2009). *Thinking in Systems: A Primer*. London, UK: Earthscan Publishing.

Miller, Arthur. (1987). *A View from the Bridge*. Directed by Alan Ayckbourn. London, UK: Royal National Theatre, Cottesloe Theatre.

Taleb, N. (2001). *Fooled by Randomness: The Hidden Role of Chance in Life and in the Markets*. Knutsford, UK: Texere Publishing Limited.

Observing 19

When a show is in tech, the stage manager and the lighting designer (and their assistant) are usually sitting in the center of the auditorium at a tech table that has been set up. The director is also usually hovering somewhere close by so as to easily speak to them. As a result, this tech table takes on a very high-status position during tech. In educational theatre, I see students vying all the time to be seated at this tech table such that in some instances the table ends up being massive to accommodate all of those that feel entitled to sit at it. Of course, the students always justify their desire by saying that they need to be next to the others to fully collaborate with them, but really it is about the status that they feel a position at that tech table will bestow upon them.

I feel bad for any director or choreographer who must approach the tech table as all these technical people are lined up behind it. It must seem at times like going before the Spanish Inquisition! Not only that but there are also mountains of technology in front of all those seated at the table, laptops, mimic screens, cue light control panels and headsets base stations, etc. To the people sitting at the tech table, this technology is important but from a director or choreographer's point of view, it represents a physical technical barrier in what should be a frictionless artistic creative process. I should imagine that even though they are probably used to it by now, it must still remain very off-putting to them.

I have tried throughout my career never to sit at that tech table.

DOI: 10.4324/9781003223160-19

For one thing, I have never felt the need to sit in a center position. Most of the audience that I am designing for are not seated in the center of the theatre so why should I need to. I am quite happy off to one side out of everyone's direct view of the stage. More importantly, I need to be somewhere where I can not only watch the stage but also watch the director, stage manager and other designers as they work. I have found that if I watch a movie with the sound off, a lot of the details that seem to get obscured by listening to the sound suddenly get revealed. Similarly, it can also be revealing watching the body language and comings and goings of the other creatives as we all work. The intelligence community refer to this as Traffic Analysis. I can tell if a problem is brewing, and I can also tell who the director thinks is driving the design at every point in the tech.

My remote outpost tech table also allows me to come and go quickly. One of the problems with the large center tech table is that with all those people sitting there and with their belongings clogging up the row of theatre seating behind, it is devilishly difficult to get in and out of. It always seems that when anyone tries to get out from sitting behind the tech table, they disturb everyone else around them. There is no chance of slipping in and out and quietly dealing with an issue without the others noticing.

Getting in and out quickly and quietly is also very important because I spend some of my time slipping into the row in front of the director where they can see me. This is important when we are running a difficult sequence that either involves sound or a sequence that is not working and may need other options discussing. As noted in chapter 10, we designers are like knights accompanying the director on our quest doing battle with the dragon. Sometimes they just need their knights beside them as moral support and as someone to bounce ideas off and discuss issues. By me coming to them rather than being stuck in a position where they must come to me, I am much more available for chance explorative creative conversations which usually translate into additional opportunities for me to design. I also believe that my freedom of movement, in comparison to the others, allows me to be viewed as much more adaptable by association with this independence and that I am much better able to quickly solve an issue[1].

Not a lot of people come and visit me at my remote outpost tech table. Most of the time this is fine as it allows me to observe the others and to get on with my just-in-time building of my cues. However, sometimes I do miss out on chance conversations. So now I implement a *honey pot*. The high-status tech table is usually laden with candies and cookies, brownies, chips (crisps) etc. In fact, because of all this junk food, usually an hour into tech most peoples' metabolism is crashing after a sugar high. Tech is so unhealthy! In consequence, I usually bring in grapes to put on my tech table. After everyone has gorged themselves on the junk food, they scour the theatre looking for an alternative and end up at my table. A couple of grapes and a quick conversation and they are happily on their way, and I have either been told something useful or have had an opportunity to ask a question or (more importantly) plant a seed of an idea in their head.

On some shows, I have taken this honey pot idea one step further. I sometimes bring in a vase of flowers to put on my tech table[2]. Unless you have worked techs, you cannot imagine how depressing it is working in darkness for weeks on end usually for eighteen hours a day. The vase of flowers becomes a bright spot in the relentless artificialness of it all. It also tends to attract people for conversations, only this time without involving any calories. As a designer, it is important to also design how and when you interact with others in your process. How to get them to come to you and when you need to go to them.

There is also another reason for my remote observation post. When we run sequences with sound (after all… I am a sound designer), I need to watch how those that are watching are physically reacting. By watching their body language and where they are looking, whether they are talking with others or focused on the stage, I can assess how engaged they are moment by moment throughout the sequence. Depending on where sound plays in the sequence of cues, I can then tell if and how much they are engaged with my sound cue. More importantly, I can usually tell at what point the sound cue started to engage them. This may be different from the point when they first heard it. Sometimes there is a kind of delayed response[3] which I need to accommodate for in the timings of my cues.

Over the years, I have realized how useless it is to ask anyone about sound cues. No one really has the language to discuss it and because it is ephemeral and time based, they usually cannot recall it after the fact, to replay the experience again in their head and comment on it accurately. Yes, they can tell me if they liked it or not, but as we have discussed at the start of this book, that is usually less than helpful. In the absence of being able to accurately interrogate the recalled experience of the sounds from their memory, they revert to an automatic response and (innocently) end up making things up that fit their preconceptions and belief about sound rather than the actuality of what happened. It is like when we convince ourselves that we are eating healthily, and then we see we have all these empty pizza boxes in our trash. Sometimes it is much better to just observe people and draw our own conclusions than to ask them.

When analyzing a character, actors learn that character is revealed by what characters do and not by what they say or is said about them. It is that difference between what they say about themselves and what is said about them, compared with their underlying character revealed by what they actually do, that sets up the tensions that drive the play. I personally have found this a very good rule to live by. I assess those around me by what they do and not what they say or is said about them.

Once the show begins invited dress rehearsals and previewing, I now have a whole audience to watch. I make sure that I am in a seat where I can not only see the show but also watch large sections of the audience. Over the years, it has become apparent to me that audiences engage with the show in two distinct ways. I call these two different ways *theatrical* and *dramatic* for want of better terms. Let me explain ….

When we observe an audience watching a show, at some moments their body language seems to include the other members of the audience sitting close to them. It is like they are experiencing the show as a member of a group rather than individually. They intermittently take quick looks to their right or left where their friends or family are sitting, to make sure the rest of their group is witnessing the same thing they are and are enjoying themselves. They also tend to lean back in their seat a little more, so they retreat into the group around them. I call this way of watching *theatrical*. When people watch a spectacle or something that is very theatrical, they seem to enjoy being part of a group watching it. It is like being at a rock concert (I'm showing my age now!). No one wants to experience a rock concert alone. It is as if we need corroboration from those around us that we are witnessing and feeling the same thing.

On the other hand, sometimes, audiences seem to be watching the show as if they are alone, as a lone fly on the wall, in a voyeuristic way. I call this way of watching *dramatic*. Their body language does not include those sitting around them. In fact, they seem almost embarrassed that others are there around them. It is as if this secret pleasure should be experienced alone. When they are watching dramatically, they seem to lean forward in their seat more in an attempt to exclude those around them from their vision and engage in a more directly focused experience.

As you can imagine, the biggest driver of whether a moment is either theatrical or dramatic in the way it resonates with an audience is acting and blocking, but design elements can also play a big part. Lighting a large spectacle and lighting a solo voyeuristic experience are two completely different things. This is not about how wide or tight the lighting is, as a pin spot can light the character of a mother clutching a child which is dramatic, and it can also be used to light a tightrope walker high up on a high wire which is theatrical. It seems to be more about the spectacle of the lighting and about lighting spill into the audience. Lighting can also make the costumes and the set more or less spectacular which also has something to do with it. Projections seem to be used theatrically more than they are used dramatically. Look up the Dallas Opera's 2010 production of *Moby Dick* and watch Elaine McCarthy's projection design on YouTube. It's a stunning piece of spectacle even though it is now over a decade ago.

It seems that it is far easier to do spectacle than it is to do drama. It is as if the visual realm is better for spectacle and sound/music is better for drama. In *The Night of the Iguana* by Tennessee Williams, we must wait a long time for one of the main characters to first enter. Usually, in a show, we get introduced to all the major characters early on while we are still in the exposition phase of a narrative. However, in *Iguana*, the character of HANNA doesn't enter until seventeen pages into the script which is quite a long way in for such a major player in the narrative. Her entrance as described in the stage directions is reproduced below.

> P17. (Shannon looks down at her, dazed. Hannah is remarkable looking-ethereal, almost ghostly. She suggests a Gothic cathedral image of a medieval saint, but animated ...)

In a production of *Iguana* that I designed the sound for, I underscored HANNAH's entrance with a beautiful musical texture like the aural equivalent of a rapture. It made for a stunning entrance as if all the oxygen had been sucked out of the room. It had the effect of turning what was up until then a theatrical experience of SHANNON stomping around the hotel and being nasty about MAXINE's breasts, and in an instant turned it into a dramatic experience of intense voyeuristic purity. My assistant and I were very pleased with the result of our cue, so much so that we felt sure that lighting had also contributed to this ethereal entrance. However, when I asked the lighting designer, he told me that HANNAH was just walking into the light of the scene and there was no additional lighting cue that was associated with her entrance. Indeed, when my assistant and I watched again more closely, we saw that was indeed the case, however, the way HANNAH entered, with her costume picking up, the light and the sound cue all around her like a fragrance or an aura, it was as if the rest of the set and actors had disappeared. It was as if we had delivered to the theatre audience the impossible; a closeup. I learned a lot from that moment as a designer.

Both ways of experiencing a show, theatrical and dramatic, are enjoyable and both are also exhausting states to remain in for too long. The more intuitive directors I have worked with understand this either consciously or unconsciously and modulate their shows so that the audience is continually going through dramatic to theatrical back to dramatic and back to theatrical repeatedly throughout the show. Once we recognize these two different types of audience engagement, we can not only build the show so that we transition between them, but we can also decide how fast or slow that transition is. In the example from *Iguana* above, the fast snap was important. HANNAH changes the dynamic of the whole play in an instant. In another production I designed the sound for, the transition took the whole show.

Beautiful Star is a Christmas play by Preston Lane with music by Laurelyn Dossett. It starts out as Appalachian humor which is very theatrical with audiences enjoying laughing together as a group and then subtly changes over the course of the show into this little dramatic jewel, intensely uplifting and innocent like a child—a baby Jesus. The smoothness of this slow transition over the whole show was very important to maintain. We could only end up at this magical moment if the audience remained unaware that we were heading in that direction and that we were taking them there with us. As a designer, once we recognize these two states of theatrical and dramatic, we can not only support them but we can make them happen. I now realize that we, as designers, are all engagement manipulators. It is just that I use sound. The sound is not important, it is the audience engagement that is.

Notes

1 I admit that I have nothing to support this assertion apart from human nature.
2 I credit the director Ashley Gates Jansen with first introducing me to this practice.
3 I have no explanation for this delay when it happens, but it does seem to be consistent each time the same scene is run.

References

Heggie, Jake & Scheer, Gene. (2010). *Moby Dick*. Directed by Leonard Foglia. Dallas, TX: The Dallas Opera, Winspear Opera House.

Lane, Preston & Dossett, Laurelyn. (2006). *Beautiful Star*. Directed by Preston Lane. Greensboro, NC: Triad Stage, The Pearl Theatre.

Williams, Tennessee. (2008). *Night of the Iguana*. Directed by Preston Lane. Greensboro, NC: Triad Stage, The Pearl Theatre.

Williams, Tennessee. (2009). *Night of the Iguana*. New York, NY: New Directions eBooks. p. 17.

Ending Safely   20

I want to discuss a couple more points before we end this... safely. The first is that as a designer, we must consider that we don't have as much time during previews to make changes as we first imagine we do. At some point before opening night, we need to hand the show back to the actors so that they have a chance to rehearse it and for it to become comfortable again for them. They need time to inhabit their character and remember what their character is now doing. Look at it from an actor's point of view. They rehearse over six weeks slowly building their characters, then they get to the stage during tech and half of what they had all that time to learn has now been changed. They really need another six weeks to integrate all these changes into their updated character before it will be resilient enough to handle opening night. Sadly, they never get the time they need, but an intuitive director will subtly start pulling back on the changes halfway through previews so that the actors (as well as the run crew) at least have a shot at becoming comfortable again.

These same directors also understand that the production is what it is. Yes, they could go on making adjustments, but at some point, they need to step back and assess what they have accomplished and just move on. In my career, I have witnessed so many opening night issues that would never have happened if the show was handed back to the actors and crew earlier.

For a designer, this means that, like the director, our design is our design. We could continue making changes and tweaking this and that, but it is time to step back and assess what we have accomplished and make note of what we will and won't do again. During these final

DOI: 10.4324/9781003223160-20

previews, even though I am pulling back on making any more major adjustments, I still like watching tech and the previews as I can also learn a lot by how the actors inhabit my design. Does my design hug the show and the characters? Is there friction? Where and what are the touch points between my design and the show? Are there any sharp points where the fit isn't good? Did I miss anything? Where am I not recognizing the *aesthetic bandwidth*[1] and needlessly doubling up on another design element. Where am I *stamping* on a moment? Where am I *gilding the lily* and should really back off? All good questions to ask yourself as a designer while watching the end product.

Two of the most important questions to ask yourself are… where am I not supporting the other design elements and where are they not supporting me? A while back, I designed the sound for Tony Kushner's adaptation of *The Illusion*. The show involves a magician living in a cave who makes illusions happen at various points. As I discussed earlier in the section about content, distribution, and environment, I like to play around with reverb a lot in my designs as I love enveloping actors and audiences in different emotional reverberant environments. Traditionally, I would have reserved the major reverb in this show for the illusions—the phantasms. However, because the magician lived in a cave and the phantasms didn't happen until much later in the show, I decided to reverb the voices of the magician and his amanuensis (servant) and the visitor, as if they were in a cave[2]. This worked for the set, as a cave is a hard thing to pull off especially if the whole idea is that it is so dark you can't see it. But when it came to the previews after I had a chance to step back and assess our production as a whole, I realized that we all had left the costume designer unsupported for the phantasms and hanging out there by themselves.

It is an illusion, so it was hard for sets to make anything magically appear quickly and then go away. Lighting lit the phantasms in an obviously different way but the more the phantasms were lit, the more the light spilled onto the cave and on to the characters watching the phantasms, so the difference was not as well defined as we were hoping for. There was also an additional issue. The characters in the phantasms were student actors from a local university whereas the other actors were professionals, cast both regionally and from New York. The student actors did a brave job but really could have used some help to redress the imbalance in experience on display. The only thing they had going for them was their costumes. The costume designer was not only one of the best I have worked with in my career (and I have worked with some truly exceptional ones), but also a friend and colleague of mine. As usual, he had done an outstanding job on this show but costumes could not on their own make the magic happen. He never complained. He is too much of a professional. But in retrospect, I could have helped him. I could have saved the live reverb for the phantasms and used a reverberant *dripping dungeon* loop for the cave instead of live reverb. This was a great lesson for me to learn. I learned that part of my job is to make *all* the other designers and the director shine!

Opening night is always an obstacle to be negotiated as a designer. Usually, our contract ends with the last afternoon tech and doesn't include the actual opening night performance. The theatre tries to sellout opening night which can also be press night (although these days with social media there is no such thing anymore). Consequently, we designers usually don't have a seat unless they are needing to *paper*[3] the performance. There is usually an opening night party afterward so we can't leave without it seeming unsupportive (although some designers do). So, what do we do?

After years of wandering the theatre hallways for the whole opening show like a stuffed lemon not knowing what to do with myself, I finally decided to *experience design* the problem. I now invite all the other designers to dinner at a local restaurant. We watch the show go up and then wander around the corner and spend a wonderful two hours having a delicious meal with lots of fascinating conversations and a few bottles of wine. We usually have no problem getting a table since the theatre crowd has just left.

By the time we have worked together, we are all way past trying to impress each other, so it is an opportunity to learn about each other as people. After all, we designers are all part of a very small community, and we need to support and care for each other, lookout for each other and enjoy each other. I have grown to love these dinners and, of course, afterwards it means we designers are the life and soul of the opening night party whereas all those others attending don't seem to initially know what to do with themselves. Unfortunately, this affirmation and support on opening night hides a dark underbelly.

I find that one of the most destructive times for any designer are the days and weeks after opening night. For months and months, we have been pushing against this large immovable mass, reforming it, and inextricably moving it with enormous effort toward opening night. Then suddenly it gives way, and the show opens, and we don't have anything more to push against.

Ending Safely 131

Did you know that tennis players also sometimes damage their arms when they miss a ball? Have you ever wondered what happens to all that energy that was being built up to transfer to the ball and send it on a winning trajectory when they miss? Where does that energy go? Well, it turns out that it is reflected back into their arm and instead of the joints and the ball absorbing it as if we had hit the ball, our ligaments, tendons, muscles now have to absorb all of that energy that didn't get transferred to the ball.

This is such a common and ubiquitous occurrence that no one takes any notice of it. But we should. It is an aspect of a well-understood phenomenon called an impedance. The basic concept is that a driver, in our case the tennis player, transfers an effort to a load, the tennis ball. This transfer of effort is measured as an amount of flow. Typically, when a driver effort is high, the driver flow is low and so the effort received by the load is low. This seems counterintuitive but think of the driver effort required when we first start to ride a bicycle. We start out putting in a lot of effort, but we only move slowly. The driver effort is impeded by the limited flow of that effort to the load. Once we have picked up some speed (a higher flow), it seems to take us less driving effort to move. However, there are limits. We can't just keep getting faster and faster ad infinitum because at some point we stop being able to pedal any faster, not because of the flow of effort to the bicycle but because of the limitations of our own driving effort. In this situation, the driving effort is low, and although the flow is high, the effort received by the load is once again being reduced. Between these two extremes, there is a sweet spot when the source impedance of our driving effort seems to match the flow impedance of effort required for the load to move. This represents the most power being transferred from us to the bicycle. This represents the highest efficiency of transfer, and this is when we describe the impedances as equally matched. (We're not saying they are the same numerical value, just that the conditions for transferring energy are ideal.)

Back to playing tennis, if the tennis ball is very heavy it would feel like a lot of effort expended on our part, but the flow would be limited so the ball would not receive much of the effort and travel very far. The driving effort that was not transferred because of constricted flow is now reflected back to us and felt as jarring and it can sometimes hurt us. A similar thing happens when the load is very light or even nonexistent as in when we miss hitting the tennis ball altogether. Any extra driving effort over and above what is required to drive this light load doesn't get received so it gets reflected back to us instead and can be jarring and potentially damaging. We call this an impedance mismatch. Impedance mismatches are not only inefficient, but we never know where that unused driving effort will end up and cause problems. We have effectively lost control of the problem.

The most destructive impedance mismatch is when a receiving load effort gets taken away suddenly. In an instant, the driving effort must be reduced to zero and the only way to do that is by infinitely high flow which is like blowing a fuse. Or conversely, if the driving effort has any momentum associated with it, it cannot instantaneously reduce to zero so it finds another load to dissipate itself on and that load may be us! This is what is happening after our design contract ends. We transition immediately from a balanced matching impedance to a catastrophic impedance mismatch.

I personally think impedance mismatch and the self-destructive power associated with it are universal and responsible for most of the human condition and not just confined to sports and the creativity of designers. What is unrequited love? It is an impedance mismatch. What is unemployment? It is an impedance mismatch. What is your party losing an election? It is an impedance mismatch. What is losing someone close? It is an impedance mismatch. What is war? It is an impedance mismatch. Maybe I need to think about writing another book!

The answer to impedance mismatches is to immediately substitute the load effort with something of equal impedance and then wind that substitute down slowly or let it dissipate slowly so that it doesn't break anything. Some designers jump headlong into another show. Some designers arrange to go on a vacation (remember... vacations are hard work! You sometimes need a vacation after a vacation to recover). Some of us jump headlong into our to-do list, or our honey-do list, or some Harry/Harriet Homeowner projects that need doing. Some of us even write books.

I am a great believer in the concept of personal art as a replacement practice. The nature of theatre is such that the creativity we practice is so sporadic, with such immense gaps and down time, that we need to develop a personal art form to fill the gaps. The reason is that if we accept Malcolm Gladwell's premise in his book *Outliers*, we all need 10,000 hours to become good at anything. If you are honest with yourself and add up how much time you do spend being creative, you will realize that you will probably die before you build up 10,000 hours. However, there is good news. If you are trying to build up your creative and innovative 10,000 hours, who is to say that those hours must only be when you are designing theatre? Maya Lin talks about this in the documentary *A Strong Clear Vision*, (1994). We see her in her art studio smashing tempered glass into a frame that she then fills with wax encapsulating the glass. She explains that the final work of art is of her height and weight. This is very different than her funerary monument designs which are dependent on other people and therefore not in her control. Whereas she can practice her personal art any time she wants to in her own studio. She doesn't even need to sell it. She just needs to practice it. She just needs to exercise her creative muscle. In fact, unlike Maya Lin, you don't even need to share your personal art. You don't need to tell anyone about it. You just need to practice it. It is YOUR personal art. YOUR private artform.

As a designer who is innovating your process of design, you need to recognize this impedance mismatch and design how you are going to overcome this. Be prepared to try many things including developing a personal art and also be prepared not to get it right the first time. Whatever end's up working for you is what will work for you. No two people are alike. However, if you ignore this part of your design process, it will always compromise your ability to evolve fully as a creative.

I hate archiving my designs. By the time I have come to the end of designing a show, you could not drag me kicking and screaming through that design again. I do however store everything. Every piece of paper along with the marked-up script, and any CDs that I burned gets put into a binder and put away on a shelf never to be touched again. Every computer file associated with the show, documents, build files and show files gets plonked in a folder on my hard drive. I even have drawers and drawers full of 3.5inch floppies, Zip disks and Jazz disks from my sampler days. And yes, I still have some reel-to-reel tape and NAB Carts hidden away in a box in the basement. I kept it all, but it was never archived. I never arranged it after the show opened so that I could find something later. That is because I have never needed to find something after I have made it. No matter if I know that I have made a similar cue before, I never go and find it in my non-archive. I always make it again from scratch. Reusing a design even if it is my own, is not the same as designing.

Having now taught many BFA and MFA sound designers over the last quarter century, I can see that some of those students, although they like being a designer, they don't seem to enjoy the process of designing. They don't like the excruciating inexactitude of it all. I, on the other hand, like designing. I like the process. I enjoy the depth of consideration, empathy and appetite for ambiguity in the work of designing. I enjoy the tightrope walk. The edge of chaos. Even the product of design as a part of the process of design interests me, but as soon as that product gets disassociated from the process of designing, I lose interest in it completely. I am not interested in remounting something that I have designed in the past. I am only interested in having another crack at the same script in a new production, but this time my fellow collaborators will be new and the ideas will be new. The audiences will even be new. I love designing! And I love redesigning the way I design!

Hopefully, if you have made it all the way to the end of this book with me, you enjoy designing too. I believe that designing deserves far more thought and experimentation with how it is done. It tends to be taught like an apprenticeship in a "design like me and you will also be a good designer" way. Even though I have used specific examples from my career as a theatre sound designer, I hope you will see this book as a license to look deeper into designing, to unlock the aspects you thought of as fixed and to redesign those aspects and the way you design. The world is changing faster and faster these days. Shouldn't the process of design also not change?

How should I design the end of a book on innovating the design process? To quote the closing monologue from the character TOM in *The Glass Menagerie* by Tennessee Williams. `"I didn't go to the moon. I went much further..."`. I encourage all of us to also go much further.

Notes

1 For an explanation of Aesthetic Bandwidth, see my paper of the same title on the USITT Sound – Research in Sound website: https://www.usitt-sound.org/2019/03/21/aesthetic-bandwidth/
2 With added textural drips and drones etc.
3 This is when theaters give away tickets to make it look like the house is fuller than had they just sold tickets.

References

Gladwell, M. (2008). *Outliers: The Story of Success*. New York, NY: Little Brown and Company.
Kushner, Tony. (2012). *The Illusion*. Directed by Preston Lane. Greensboro, NC: Triad Stage, The Pearl Theatre.
Lee Mock, F. (Director) & Sanders, T. (Producer). (1994). *Maya Lin: A Strong Clear Vision* [Motion Picture]. Washington, DC: American Film Foundation.
Williams, T. (1944). *The Glass Menagerie*. New York, NY: Random House Play. First line of TOM's final soliloquy.

Index

10,000 hours 132
1000 different sound elements 98
3.5inch floppies 133

Abramovic, Marina 1
academic year 74
acclimatization 89
accolades 101
actuality 123
adaptability 38, 82, 104–5, 116–8
additive synthesis 104
adjustments 34, 115, 128–9
advertising 62
aesthetic bandwidth 108, 129
aesthetic context 115–6
affirmation 130
agile 13, 20, 23, 26, 54, 71, 82, 108
Albert Bridge 24
amanuensis 129
ambiguity 2, 133
analogue 12, 67, 71
analogue synthesizers 104
Angels in America 93
angle grinding 111
Anna Christie 92
annoy 76
anthropological 11
Antikythera 21

Appalachian 126
apprenticeship, 134
architectural 39
archive 24, 133
Arena Stage 23
armor 69
armories 34
art galleries 71
artificialness 123
artistry 111
assess 10, 37, 108, 119, 123–4, 128
attention 8, 43, 51, 81, 91–3, 105, 112
audience attention 112
audience engagement 126
aura 125
authenticity 106
automatic design process 7–8
automatic response 53, 123
automation 74; *see also* MoCo
Avnet, Jon 77
Ayckbourn, Alan 26, 116

baggage 10, 30, 43
balance 113, 115, 119
balanced matching impedance 132
bandwidth 19
Barnard, Rob 116
Barney, William 66–8

bass guitar 77
bath 119
be prepared 133
Beautiful Star 126
BFA 1, 4, 133
bicycle 131
big picture 18, 67
Black Mountain College 1
black-box 10
blocking 42, 124
blowing a fuse 132
body language 105, 122–4
bold 52, 63, 87, 91, 94
Borders Books 69
brainstormed 53
brainstorming 11–14
bravest directorial moment 53
breaks the cycle 118
Bruce Tick 24, 33
Bruce, Andrew 99
Bryant, Michael 22
bugs 39
build files 133
button 38

cacophony 29, 114
calories 123
candy store 24; *also see* sweetshop
carburetors 22
cardboard 10
care for each other 130
career 3–5, 15, 36–7, 39, 53, 65, 73, 86, 98–101, 110–1, 114, 120–1, 128–9, 134
cart 117, 133
cartoonish 88
Cat on a Hot Tin Roof 81–2, 86, 88, 95
catastrophic impedance mismatch 132
cats 42–3
cave 129–30
CD 37, 76, 133
cell phone conversations 112
central essence 32–3
chaise 54
character emerges 71
character motivation 22
chemist 59

cherry picker 111
chewed out 114
child (parent/child) 24, 26, 30, 34, 45
child 5, 61, 81, 124, 126
childlike 23
children 6, **87**
chip away 34–5
chips (crisps) 122
choirboy 38
choreograph 105
choreographer 4, 121
choreography 21
A Chorus of Disapproval 23
chosen few 65
Christmas 89, 126
Church bells 28–9
Cirque du Soleil 76
city planner 61
Civil Rights Memorial 7, 8
class 1–4, 7, 65, 69–70, 65
clipping 111
closeu, 67, 125
coffee 19, 69–70, 114
cogs 21, 47, 63
collaborate(ion) 8–10, 12–13, 16–18, 20, 47, 68, 108, 121
collapse 45, 59–60, 69, 97, 108
colleague 77, 130
comedic 41–2
complex(ity) 21–22, 58–9, 80, 85, 96, 101, 91
composer 33, 77
computer file 133
concept 12, 16, 28, 33, 38–9, 53, 55, 61, 104–5, 108, 131–2
conceptual artists 3, 5
conceptual essence 38
conceptually group 105
connotations 30, 43, 48
conservatory 1, 65
consideration 2, 133
constricted flow 131
consumer 62
content 21–2, 56, 104–8, 112–3, 117, 129
context 15, 31–2, 76, 88, 115–6
continuous partial attention 92
contract 7, 9, 19, 73, 77, 84, 130, 132

Index

contribution 9, 22, 41, 56, 74–5, 83, 101, 108, 112, 115–6, 119, 106, 107, 114, 125
conversation(s) 2, 4, 13, 33, 42, 44, 48, 52, 88, 109, 110, 116, 123
cookies 122
cool 62–3, 65, 67
copy and paste 48
corroboration from those around us 124
costed out 74
costume designer(s) 8, 29, 36, 116, 118, 129
costume(s) 8, 22, 29–31, 36, 41, 73–4, 102, 107, 115–8, 125, 129, 130
Cottesloe Theatre 116
counterintuitive 131
creative conversations 122
The Creative Habit 4
creative muscle 61, 133
creative practitioners 65
creative process 1–3, 5, 7–8, 12–3, 18–19, 65, 108, 117, 121
credible 7, 32, 60
crickets 89
Crime on the Orient Express 22
criticism 11
croquet 88–9
crossovers 115
crystals 59–60, 62
Csikszentmihalyi, M. 3
Cue-to-Cue 102
cultural terrain 71
cutting of cues 41–2, 56, 86, 108
Cymbeline 22

D&P 74
D2 5
Dallas Opera 125
damping 119
dark underbelly 130
DAT tape recorders 100
Deans, Jonathan 76
Deep Dive 11
delay 104, 118–9
delayed response 123
Dennett, Daniel 62

denotation 30
Design and Production 74
design presentations 4, 73
design proposals 116
design quiet time 110–1, 113
design skills 11
Design squared 5
designed experience 10
designer run 18, 38, 71, 73, 79, 81–6, 99, 110–11
Designing design 5
designing leeway 116
destruction of resources 62
destructive 130, 132
developing a design 67
Dial 'M' for Murder 77
dials 21–2
different reality 81
difficult sequence 122
ding 28–30
dinner 19, 130
directing the audience's attention 92
disappeared (actors) 125
discard 61–3
dispensing machine 107
distorting, 111
distribution, 104–8, 112, 117
documentary(ies) 1, 7–8, 10, 65, 132
dog bark 89, 99–101, 107
doorbell 30, 100–1
dopamine 2
Dossett, Laurelyn 126
double-blind 30
Dracula 38
dragon, 69, 122
drama 13, 24, 67, 78, 92, 125
dramatic 124–6
dramaturges 19, 73
drawers 133
dress rehearsal 92, 118, 124
driver effort 131–2
drum road 116
dry sound 106
Dry-Tech 102–3
due diligence 47, 58
dues 74
dynamic range 110

Eames 1
eating healthily 123
EccoPro 24, 39
edge of chaos 108, 133
editing sounds 13
educational theatre 121
educator(s) 4, 17, 65, 74, 84
election 132
Elysian Fields 49, 52–3
Emanating (sound) 112
embarrassed 124
emotional 31, 56, 94, 107, 112, 129
emotional underscores 112
empathy 2, 11, 81, 113
end-product 9, 13, 75, 129
ending points 81
energy 131
engaged 92, 118, 123
engagement 8, 75, 94, 126
engineering 5
Enigmagic 111
enigmatic magic making 111
enjoy designing 36, 134
enjoy each other 130
entitled 121
entrances 115
enveloping actors and audiences 129
environment 52, 55, 104, 106–8, 112, 117, 129
environments 107, 129
ephemeral 33, 123
equal impedance 132
Equity 82–4
essence 1, 7, 20, 32–3, 37–8, 53, 73, 94
essential 37–8
ethereal entrance 125
Excel 86, 98
exhausting 75, 126
exits 115, 118
experience design 130
experimental artists 3, 5

fabric 8, 37, 116
fade-down 93
fade-in 93
fade-out 93
fade-up 93

fans 112–3
feather 105
feathers 36
feedback 118–9
felt bad 115
ferment 83
Feynman, Richard 59
Fichandler 23
fidelity 111, 114
filler 37
filtering 24, 104
financial risk 69
fireworks 81, 95–6
first stab 74
fittings 73, 117
Flow (Csikszentmihalyi) 3
flow 63, 105, 118–9, 131–2
fluid 20, 70, 101
fly on the wall 124
foam-core 10, 14, 16, 73
FOH 110
folder 133
Fooled by Randomness 116
form finding 8, 19
Form vs Content 21
formula one race 118
fragrance 125
freight train 43, 52
friction 115, 117, 129
frictionless 121
Fried Green Tomatoes 77
friend 30, 130
frogs 106
front of house, 110
frustration 114
funerary monument 133

Galenson, David 3, 5
Gambon, Michael 116
GEB Triplet 32
Gehry, Frank 10
Gelato 20
Genie 111
Geraldine James 22
Gerhardt Richter 1
gift 65, 69
gilding the lily 129

Girl on a Train 52
gives way 130
Gladwell, Malcolm 132
The Glass Menagerie 55, 57, 134
Glennie, Evelynne 1
go up 130
goal, 33 119
Gödel, Escher, Bach 32, 34
Goldsworthy, Andy 1
grammar 58, 63
granular 38–9, 59
granularity 36–7, 80
granularization 82
grapes 123
grass 39
gravel 39
Groothuis, Paul 104
gunshot 81
Guo-Qiang, Cai 1
Gymkhana 24

Hall, Peter 22
handed back to the actors 128
hard copy 79
hard drive 133
Haystackness 12
headphones 77, 114
helicopter 100
Hemming, Lindy 116
Henderson, Shirley 22
high school 55, 92
high wire 125
high-status 121–2
highest efficiency of transfer 131
Hill, Susan 94
Hofstadter, Douglas 32
honey pot 122–3
honey-do list 132
hot mess 117
hug 37, 105, 129
human condition 132
hums and buzzes 110
hurt us 131

IDEO 9, 11–2, 14, 16, 18, 36
The Illusion 129
illusions 129

imagination 9, 12–3, 15
immense gaps 132
immersion 104
immovable mass 130
impedance 131–3
implementation process 38, 73, 79, 104, 108
implementing a design 4, 82, 111
impress 130
incompetence 110
industrial 9
inflows 119
information 23–4, 26, 39, 45–6, 79, 86, 99, 119
Inge, William 38
ingredients 71, 83
inhabit my design 129
inhabit their character 128
innate talent 65
innocent 123, 126
Innovation and Creativity 1, 3–5, 7, 65, 69
intention 33, 38, 40, 47–8, 56
interact with others 123
interconnectedness 71
interrogate the recalled experience 123
intuitive directors 126
invited dress 124
is what it is 10, 128
issues 14, 102, 110–1, 115, 122
iterations 13

James, Geraldine 22
jarring 131
Jazz Band 43, 56
Jazz disks 133
Jesus 126
jewel 126
joints 70, 131
Jones, Howard 39
journey 3, 8, 19, 23, 33–4, 65, 67, 71, 75–6, 89, 99
journeying 70
judge 5, 23
juggling 103
junk food 122–3
justification 22, 38, 44–5, 48, 58, 63

Kahn, Louis 1
Kansas 39
Kazan, Elia 88
Kerner, Jordan 77
knights 69, 122
known knowns 116
known unknown 116
Kushner, Tony 93, 129

labor intensive 10
ladder 100, 112
Lane, Preston 38, 45, 53, 61, 126
laptop 13, 58, 77, 114
last iteration 119
laughing together 126
lean back in their seat 124
learning process 61, 102
Lee, Robert Charles 98
Lembridge Tennit 24
levels 68, 102, 107, 113
levers 21, 47
library 36, 98–9
ligaments 131
lighting 8, 12, 23, 31, 41, 48, 73–5, 85, 87, 91, 95–6, 99, 102, 105, 107, 111–2, 121, 124–5, 129
lighting spill 125
like it 31, 48, 86, 106, 108
Lin, Maya 7–8, 12, 14, 132–3
Lincoln, Abraham 4
local restaurant 130
London 37
longshoreman 117
lookout for each other 130
looks 48, 74, 105
loops 80–1, 119
losing someone close 132
lost control 91, 94, 132
Loud sounds in the house 112
Louvre 71
love 10, 111, 129–30, 132, 134
luxuriate 60, 108

Mac 39
machine 21, 26, 47, 56, 107
magazine 54, 69–71

magic sheets 105
magical moment 126
malevolent 41
Mallatratt, Stephen 94
management 2, 17, 19, 53, 114–5
marathon 70
marching music 78
Mardi Gras 43, 56
marked-up script 133
McCarthy, Elaine 125
McCartney, Paul 77
meal 130
meaning/feeling 43–4, 52, 55, 56
Meet & Greet 10, 73–8, 83
metabolism 122
metaphor 21
MFA 1, 4, 133
milestone 60
military highway 22
Miller, Arthur 116
mimed 42, 92
misfits 31
miss anything 79, 129
Miss Saigon 99–100
Moby Dick 125
MoCo 102; *also see* Motion Control
models 8, 10–1, 14, 16, 73, 75
modulate 126
mold 24
momentary 44, 71
momentum 75, 132
Monet, C. 12
monologue 89, 134
Montague 29
moon 134
moral support 122
more or less spectacular 125
Moscow 22
Motion Control 91
Mount Olympus 67
movie 31, 77, 99, 122
Muertos Flores 54
Muganga, Lawrence 65
muscles 70, 131
Muse 26, 63, 67
Musée d'Orsay 71
Museums 71

Index

music 20, 22–4, 31, 33, 38, 52, 54, 57, 67, 76–8, **86**, 88, 94, 104–5, 111–2, 114, 125–6
musical texture 125
muslin 8, 10, 15

NAB cartridge 117, 133
Nailed to 94–5
National Geographic 71
needless friction 115, 117
Newman, Thomas 77
nice person 75, 100
night before 89, 111
The Night of the Iguana 88, 125
noise 41, 44, 50, 77, 84, 104, 110, 113
not supporting 129

O'Neill, Eugene 67, 92
objet d'art 10
Observe, 1–3 108, 122–4
Odysseus 67
The Odyssey 66–8
The Odyssey Timeline 66, 68
Old Masters and Young Geniuses 3
on the same page 75
on-ramp 67
one step behind 119
opening night 39, 58, 75, 128, 130
opening night party 130
opinion 2–3, 47, 67, 100, 111
opportunities 19, 60, 81, 84–5, 115, 122
optimization 61–3
options 11, 13, 38, 62, 122
oscillations 119
Our Town 92
outflows 119
Outliers 132
overcompensating 119
overreact 119
overshoot 119
owl hoot 81
own studio 133
ownership 9, 12–3
Oxford English Dictionary 98
oxygen 125

page number 45, 48
pageant queen 81
paint crew, 111
paints 111–2
pallet 31
pantomime 101
paper a performance 130
paperboy 54–5
paperwork 74–5
parent 24, 30, 34, 46
parent/child 24, 30, 46
Paris Match 71
Perception 11, 77, 94
perfect 32–3, 35, 108
personal art 132–3
perspective(s) 1, 11, 33, 110
phantasms 129–30
Photoshop 8
physically reacting 123
Picasso 1
Picnic 38
Pigott-Smith, Tim 22
pin spot 124
pizza 123
planning and intention 33
plant a seed 123
Plantagenet King, 19
playing space 74
playwright 21, 23, 47, 49, 56
plots 74–5, 99
podcast 78
politics 119
Pollack, Sydney 10
Pompidou Center 71
pony and skip 95
population growth 119
portfolio 74
post-it notes 11–2, 14, 36, 67–8
pre analysis 22
pre class 70
pre prototype 17–8, 20, 53, 75
precious 9–11, 13, 53, 111
preconceptions 123
prerecorded 80–1
presentational 67
presentational persistence 14
previews 80, 124, 128–9

priorities 92
private messaging 19
privately confirm 117
process of designing 13, 16–7, 133
production elements 22, 96, 103, 112
projection 42, 85, 91, 117, 125
projections 8, 41, 73–4, 85, 102, 125
props 10, 36, 38, 48, 102, 115, 118
provisional sound design 24–6
pull back 55, 128–9
purity 20, 125
push against 130
pyro **96**

quantum physics 59
Quest 59, 69, 122
quiet theatre 102, 111

rabbit holes 70
raffish charm 49, 52–3, 55
randomness 116
rape 45, 54
rapture 125
rat 38
readthrough 73, 78, 82–3
reconstruct 38, 108
record 24, 100, 106, 117
recordings 24, 37, 98
Recreation 5, 39
redesign 134
redundancy 41
reel to reel 117, 133
reflected back 131
reflection 2, 19, 114
regional theatre 45, 73, 79, 84, 111
rehearsal process 17, 74, 80
rehearsal room 19, 21, 82
rehearsals 11, 17, 73–4, 116, 124
remounting 134
rendering(s) 8–9, 67, 73
replay the experience 123
reproducible process 23, 69
research 11, 45–7, 49–50, 52, 54, 58–9, 63, 69
resilient 23, 26, 31, 63, 128
resistance 13
respond 18,31, 65, 101–2, 108

retrospect 130
return carriage bell 26, 28–9
The Revengers' Comedies 23–6
The Revengers' Comedies Provisional Sound Design *25*
reverb 54, **86**–8, 106–7, 129–30
Richter, Gerhardt 1
rigged 74, 86, 110
rigor(ous) 65, 69, 84
river 49
riveter 52
RNT 22, 37, 100, 116
Robinson, Ken 65
rock concert 124
Roland synthesizer 100
role 14, 19, 22, 75
Romeo and Juliet 29
Rosetta Stone, 68
Rosie the riveter 52
rough prototypes 9, 11
Royal National Theatre 22, 37, 100, 116
rumination 2, 19, 83
Russians 22

sampler 117, 133
Saxton-Billing 24
scale 9–10, 67, 77
scene change 45, 54–7, 105, 112
Scenic (scene) designers 73–4, 84; *see also* Set designer
scheduling meetings 111
Schlamme, Thomas 95
scratch 37, 59, 61–3, 99, 133
scratching 59–60, 89
scribble(s) 79–82
script analysis 22–3, 33, 47
seams 116
second world war 52
secret pleasure 124
Semiotics 28
serving a show 67
set designer(s) 8, 10–11, 39, 75
settle down 101
SFX CD 37
Shakespeare 22, 29, 93
shaming 74
sharp points 129

shine 130
shopkeeper's bell 26, 28–9
shorthand 80
show files 133
show monitor 86
Shutt, Christopher 100
signify 12, 28–30, 48, 54, 89
silence 89, 93
silk pajamas 45
simplicity 59–60, 69
Simulated Annealing 62–3
six weeks 128
size of the world 112
skeptical person 23
Sketches of Frank Gehry 10
Skywalker 31, 33
slipping in and out 122
small community 130
smoke/haze **96**
snap 93, 126
snug 37
social media 2, 19, 130
soft goods hamper 95
software 24, 40, 46
solidarity 75
soliloquy 81, 88
Sony 77
Sorkin, Aaron 95
sound crappy 76
sound stands in for the *thing* 99
sound technician/engineer 14
soundscape(s) 29, 106
Soviet 22
spaceship 61
Spanish Inquisition 121
specials 74, 99
spectacle 124–5
spelling 58
sporadic 132
sports 5, 88, 132
spreadsheet 86, 95–6, 98
stage crew 111, 114–5
stage direction(s) 23, 44–5, 47–8, 51, 54, 84, 88, 110, 125
stage manager(s) 17–9, 73, 84–7, 95–6, 98, 114–5, 121–2
stamping on 81, 129

Star Wars 31
starting point(s) 69, 81, 113
steal attention 22, 43, 91–3
stealing like an artist 1
step back 53, 128–9
stereotype 65, 69
stimulus 69, 91
Stingray 61
stocks 119
stop tech 117
store everything 133
streamlined passenger service 51–2, 55
A Streetcar Named Desire 41, 45, 53, 56, 47, 61
A Strong Clear Vision 7, 132
stuck time 118
student's point of view 4
student(s) 1–4, 17, 22, 30, 55–6, 61, 65, 67, 69, 70, 73–4, 80–1, 84, 99,–100, 121, 129, 133
stuffed lemon 130
sub bass 94
submarine 61
subtractive 104
sugar high 122
suit up 59, 69, 71
surreal 54, 81
swapping out cables 111
swatches 8, 73
swatted 39
sweet shop 24, 26, 28
symbol 12–3, 28–30, 37–8, 44, 45, 52, 54
sync 60
synesthetic 42
system quiet time 110–1
systems 5, 116, 119
systems thinking 119

tagging 24, 30
take sides 115
Taleb, Nassim Nicholas 116
Tbilisi 22
TCG 93
team 1, 3, 10–2, 53–4, 69, 71, 74, 95, 99–100, 113–5
team building 114

team dynamics 114
team-teach 3
tease 45
teasing 74
tech table 121–3
technical barrier 121
technology 5, 117, 121
telephone 45, 56, 112
telling the story 84, 91, 101, 112
tempered glass 132
The Tempest 22
template(s) 46, 48–9, 106–7, 112–3, 118
tendons 131
tennis ball 131
tension(s) 22, 42, 44, 54, 101, 124
textural 39
Tharp, Twyla 1, 4–5
theatre hallways 130
theatre sound 4, 94, 134
theatrical 45, 124–6
theory 12, 15, 108
thought and experimentation 134
three-dimensional 105
The three stages of designing a show 16–8
Thunderbirds 61
thunderstorm 54
thwonk 100
tightrope 108, 125, 133
time based 67, 82, 91, 123
Time-Life 71
timeline 66–9, 73
tinkle 26, 29
tires 39
to-do list 132
Top of the show **86**, 102, 105, 112
touch points 129
touch-up time 111
tracing signals 111
track titles 37
train 41–4, 49–50, 52, 55–6, 58
transfer to the ball 131
transformational 9
transition 16–8, 20, 45, 74, 105–6, 115, 126, 132

Triad Stage 38, 45
trial-and-error 12
triangle 106
trucks 22, 39
trust 61, 76
turbo fan engine 100
turf 39
typewriter 24, 26, 28–9, 33

ubiquitous, 112, 131
UK 23
UNCSA 1, 17, 60, 74,
under adapting 119
unemployment 132
unhealthy 123
unification 59
United Scenic Artists 73
universal 15–6, 54, 75, 132
university 1, 4, 24, 129
unlock 5, 16, 134
unrequited 132
unsupported 129
uplifting 126

vacation 81, 132
vacuuming 114
Varsouvianna 54
vase of flowers 123
vending machine 107
verbal 7–8, 12, 14
verbatim 45, 48
verboten 112
video recording 82
videoconference 19
Vietnam Veterans Memorial 7–8
View (Blanche's) 53
View (narrative & vocabuary) 24,26, 32–5, 39, 46, 54, 71
A View from the Bridge 116
vigilant 115
Vignellis 1
vision 73, 75–6, 124
vocabulary(ies) 31–4, 39, 54, 58–9, 63, 69, 71, 78, 80–1, 84–6, 88, 98–99, 101, 107, 112
voyeuristic 124–5

Wager, Doug 23
Waiting for sound 74, 117
Walk and Talk 95
walkers 102
war 52, 132
Warhorse 100
warm up 69–71
waste, 62 116
watercolorists 105
waves 92
wax 133
Webb, Craig 10
West End 99
wet 106, 112
Whale 100
what they do 2, 124
White House 95
whiteboard 46
Wigs 22, 37
Wilder, Thornton 92
Williams, John 31, 33

Williams, Tennessee 41, 81, 125, 134
wind 37, 89, 106, 132
wine 94, 130
winners or losers 5
winning trajectory 131
winnowing process 32, 84
The Winter's Tale 22
witnessing the same thing 124
The Woman in Black 94–5
world is changing 120
wrapper(s) 107–8
writings 5, 63

You Can't Make Fish Climb Trees 65
YouTube 125
Yugoslavia 22

zero to one 85
Zimmerman, Mary 67
Zip disks 133

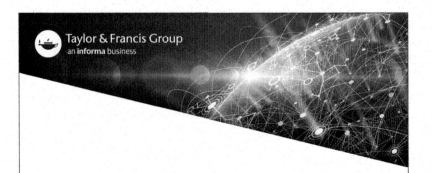